The Indian Reservation System

Other Books in the At Issue in History Series:

The Indian Reservation System

Terry O'Neill, *Book Editor*

Daniel Leone, *Publisher*
Bonnie Szumski, *Editorial Director*
Scott Barbour, *Managing Editor*

OPPOSING
VIEWPOINTS®
SERIES

AT ISSUE IN HISTORY

Greenhaven Press, Inc.
San Diego, California

No part of this book may be reproduced or used in any form or by any means, electrical, mechanical, or otherwise, including, but not limited to, photocopy, recording, or any information storage and retrieval system, without prior written permission from the publisher.

Library of Congress Cataloging-in-Publication Data

The Indian reservation system / Terry O'Neill, book editor.
        p.   cm. — (At issue in history)
     Includes bibliographical references and index
     ISBN 0-7377-0714-3 (pbk. : alk. paper) —
ISBN 0-7377-0715-1 (lib. : alk. paper)
     1. Indian reservations—United States—History.
2. Indian reservations—Government policy—United States.
3. Indians of North America—Relocation. 4. Indians of North America—Government relations. I. O'Neill, Terry, 1944–
II. At issue (San Diego, Calif.)
E93 .I3827 2002
323.1'197073—dc21

2001023818

© 2002 by Greenhaven Press, Inc., PO Box 289009,
San Diego, CA 92198-9009

Printed in the U.S.A.

Contents

A well-known clergyman maintains that the reservation system is not civilizing the Indians, and it is holding back whites who could be using the reservation lands fruitfully. The reservation system should be ended.

Chapter 4: Seesaw in the Twentieth Century (1934–1999)

Foreword

Historian Robert Weiss defines history simply as "a record and interpretation of past events." Both elements—record and interpretation—are necessary, Weiss argues.

Names, dates, places, and events are the essence of history. But historical writing is not a compendium of facts. It consists of facts placed in a sequence to tell a connected story. A work of history is not merely a story, however. It also must analyze what happened and *why*—that is, it must interpret the past for the reader.

For example, the events of December 7, 1941, that led President Franklin D. Roosevelt to call it "a date which will live in infamy" are fairly well known and straightforward. A force of Japanese planes and submarines launched a torpedo and bombing attack on American military targets in Pearl Harbor, Hawaii. The surprise assault sank five battleships, disabled or sank fourteen additional ships, and left almost twenty-four hundred American soldiers and sailors dead. On the following day, the United States formally entered World War II when Congress declared war on Japan.

These facts and consequences were almost immediately communicated to the American people who heard reports about Pearl Harbor and President Roosevelt's response on the radio. All realized that this was an important and pivotal event in American and world history. Yet the news from Pearl Harbor raised many unanswered questions. Why did Japan decide to launch such an offensive? Why were the attackers so successful in catching America by surprise? What did the attack reveal about the two nations, their people, and their leadership? What were its causes, and what were its effects? Political leaders, academic historians, and students look to learn the basic facts of historical events and to read the intepretations of these events by many different sources, both primary and secondary, in order to develop a more complete picture of the event in a historical context.

In the case of Pearl Harbor, several important questions surrounding the event remain in dispute, most notably the role of President Roosevelt. Some historians have blamed his policies for deliberately provoking Japan to attack in order to propel America into World War II; a few have gone so far as to accuse him of knowing of the impending attack but not informing others. Other historians, examining the same event, have exonerated the president of such charges, arguing that the historical evidence does not support such a theory.

The Greenhaven At Issue in History series recognizes that many important historical events have been interpreted differently and in some cases remain shrouded in controversy. Each volume features a collection of articles that focus on a topic that has sparked controversy among eyewitnesses, contemporary observers, and historians. An introductory essay sets the stage for each topic by presenting background and context. Several chapters then examine different facets of the subject at hand with readings chosen for their diversity of opinion. Each selection is preceded by a summary of the author's main points and conclusions. A bibliography is included for those students interested in pursuing further research. An annotated table of contents and thorough index help readers to quickly locate material of interest. Taken together, the contents of each of the volumes in the Greenhaven At Issue in History series will help students become more discriminating and thoughtful readers of history.

Introduction

Almost from the day European settlers set foot in the New World, trouble began between them and the Indians. It was inevitable, for the settlers came to America with the explicit expectation of acquiring and exploiting land and natural resources; yet 1.5 million Indians had inhabited the continent for centuries and wished to continue using the land in the ways they had been.

The Indians, generally, did not have the same concept of private land ownership that the European settlers did. Historian Eric Mayer notes, "Indians did not see land as a source of profit as many European individuals and business concerns did, but rather as the direct source of life. The vast majority of native people had no concept of private ownership of land. Lands and the right to use them were held by entire communities or extended kin groups."[1] In many instances, the Indians were willing to share the use of their lands with the settlers, but this did not satisfy the settlers. They established towns and farms and individual ownership of parcels of the land. At times, the settlers completely overran the territory of certain tribes and forced them to move out. As early as 1637, the Puritans battled the Pequots, claiming jurisdiction over their territory and ultimately forcing the Pequots onto a 1,200-acre land parcel—a foreshadowing of the reservations to come.

In some instances, Indians and the European settlers were able to live in harmony, but as more settlers came, claiming more land as their own, conflict grew. During the colonization period, William Canby Jr. reports,

> The British Crown dealt with the Indian tribes formally as foreign sovereign nations. Britain and several of its colonies entered treaties with various tribes. As the colonies grew in strength and population, it became apparent that individual colonists were encroaching upon Indian lands and were otherwise treating the Indians unfairly or worse. In order to avoid prolonged and ex-

pensive Indian wars, and perhaps also to enforce a measure of justice, the Crown increasingly assumed the position of protector of the tribes from the excesses of the colonists. It is accordingly not surprising that when the colonies revolted from Britain, nearly all of the tribes allied themselves with the Crown.[2]

It was an unfortunate choice by the Indians, for many of the former colonists did not think well of the "savages" who had fought against them.

Beginnings of Indian Policy

Once the new nation established its own government, it began to develop policies to deal with the Indians. It enacted a series of Trade and Intercourse Acts meant to govern relations between the two factions. Historian Francis Paul Prucha, author of numerous historical studies of Indian-white relations, writes that by the 1830s, the United States had "determined a set of principles which became the standard base lines of American Indian policy."[3] Prucha writes that the acts established six fundamentals:

1) Protection of Indian rights to their land by setting definite boundaries for the Indian Country, restricting the whites from entering the area except under certain controls, and removing illegal intruders.

2) Control of the disposition of Indian lands by denying the right of private individuals or local governments to acquire land from the Indians by purchase or by any other means.

3) Regulation of the Indian trade by determining the conditions under which individuals might engage in the trade, prohibiting certain classes of traders, and actually entering into the trade itself.

4) Control of the liquor traffic by regulating the flow of intoxicating liquor into the Indian Country and then prohibiting it altogether.

5) Provision for the punishment of crimes committed by members of one race against the other and compensation for damages suffered by one group at the hands of the other, in order to remove the occasions for private retaliation which led to frontier hostilities.

6) Promotion of civilization and education among the Indians, in the hope that they might be absorbed into the general stream of American society.[4]

Sovereign No More

In 1828, Andrew Jackson was elected president. He and other members of the government believed that the Trade and Intercourse Acts had failed to adequately deal with "the Indian problem." Among Jackson's constituents were wealthy southern landowners who wanted to expand their plantations into lands occupied by the Indians. Jackson shared their perspective and helped set in motion the first great "removals" of Indians from the lands the federal government had guaranteed them.

There had been previous instances in which tribes had been moved off their lands, either through negotiated purchases or by force, but none as large as the ones that began under Jackson's administration. In 1828, the Georgia state legislature granted itself greater power over the Cherokee by asserting that the Indians could not maintain sovereign nations within a state's boundaries; they had no rights to self-governance or even to ownership of the lands formerly guaranteed them by treaty.

Georgia's U.S. senators also introduced the Indian Removal Bill, which passed in 1830. This law established federal policy to move all the tribes of the southeastern United States westward to new lands beyond the Mississippi River. This left the rich, southern soil free for cotton and tobacco plantations and sent the Indians to a newly established Indian Territory—today the states of Oklahoma, Kansas, and Arkansas. Thought to be little more than desert at that time, the land was assumed to be of no interest to white settlers. The establishment of this Indian Territory, says historian Judith Nies, "was the forerunner of the reservation system."[5]

A lawsuit on behalf of the Cherokee nation against the state of Georgia was decided in favor of the Cherokee, who did not want to move, but the decision had no effect on either President Jackson or the state of Georgia. Reportedly, Jackson said, "[U.S. Supreme Court chief justice] John Marshall has made his decision, now let's see him enforce it."[6] And so in the winter of 1838 began the tragic migration known as the Trail of Tears, in which sixteen thousand Cherokee began the

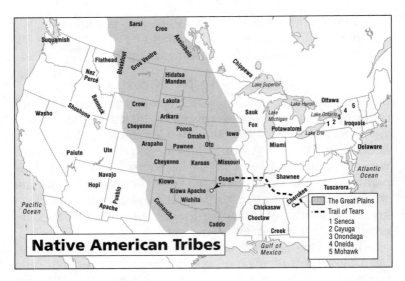

Native American Tribes

walk from their homes in Georgia to the new Indian Territory in Oklahoma. They were accompanied by seven thousand federal troops and uncounted Georgia militia. During
the six-month trek, some four thousand Cherokee died.

Reservations Are Born

In the first half of the nineteenth century, more than
100,000 Indians were removed from their lands and relocated to areas thought to be of little interest to white settlers—either less desirable areas within a state or to Indian
Territory and other places west.

The removals forced a whole new way of life on the Indians. Indians who had been accustomed to traversing hundreds or even thousands of miles over the course of a year
were now confined to reservations of several hundred or a
few thousand acres. Tribes who had nothing in common—
and may even have been traditional enemies—were placed in
the same territory. Often the lands the Indians were moved to
had little resemblance to where they had lived before. Tribes
who had roamed and hunted amidst hills and forests might be
removed to barren desert or rocky canyons. Ten Bears, a Co-
manche chief, expressed a common Indian view of the removals to reservations: "I was born upon the prairie, where
the wind blew free, and there was nothing to break the light
of the sun. I was born where there were no enclosures, and
where everything drew a free breath. I want to die there, and
not within walls. . . . Why do you ask us to leave the rivers,

and the sun, and the wind, and live in houses? Do not ask us to give up the buffalo for the sheep."[7]

Not only the land was different. Generally, government policy was aimed at getting the Indians to abandon age-old beliefs and traditions and replace them with something more akin to the new Americans' customs. William Canby Jr. writes that "Reservations were originally intended to keep distance and peace between Indians and non-Indians, but they came to be viewed also as instruments for 'civilizing' the Indians. Each reservation was placed in the charge of an Indian agent whose mission was to supervise the Indian's adaptation to non-Indian ways."[8] Indian children were sent away to boarding schools to learn white language, skills, and values. Indian religious practices were banned. During one period late in the century, Christian missionaries were made the official Indian agents, and they did their best to convert the "heathen savages" to "civilized Christianity."

The Reservation System Is Destroyed

As drastic a change as the reservations were, worse was to come. A combination of good and bad intentions led to the 1887 Dawes Act, also known as the General Allotment Act. It had a disastrous effect on the Indians.

The good intentions were held by people who considered themselves friends of the Indians—in fact, a prominent organization, whose members were exclusively white, called itself Friends of the Indians. These people saw how the reservations had turned out to be poverty- and disease-ridden prisons. They believed that the Indians' lives could be turned around if they simply learned to live and think like whites, which they were not doing on the reservations. As one Indian agent reported, "As long as Indians live in villages they will retain many of their old and injurious habits. Frequent feasts, heathen ceremonies and dances, constant visiting—these will continue."[9] Despite the best efforts of Indian agents and missionaries, the Indians tended to remain tribe-centered. People friendly to the Indians thought that a key factor to changing this was private land ownership. If Indians owned their own plot of land, they would become successful farmers, they would give up their "primitive" communal lifestyles, and they would assume the American dream of individualism and material success.

The bad intentions leading to the Dawes Act were held by those who saw the reservations as containing a lot of land that could be better used by white settlers.

These two factions came together to promote the end of the reservation system, which was the aim of the Dawes Act. The act ended tribal government and broke up reservation land into 160-acre parcels that were allotted to individual families. (Actually, the land was assigned to the Indians, but the government held title to it for twenty-five years. This was to prevent the Indians from squandering their property or from being swindled out of it while they were still naive to the ways of capitalism.) Any land that was not allotted in this manner was available to be sold by the government to white settlers. This was thought to be an additional benefit of the law: Now Indians would be living and working side by side with whites and would have a better opportunity to learn how to be successful in America.

Within a few years of its implementation, it was clear that allotment was a failure. The Indians had not adapted well to a tribeless society; many were unable to eke out even the barest existence on the land that had been allotted to them; and they had not integrated into white society. Instead, both their lands and their populations were decimated. During the allotment period, Indians lost another 90 million acres of land, and their population plunged from an estimated 1.5 million at the time of the first settlers to 237,000 in 1900.

Reservations Rise Again

Reformers began to see that Indians did best when they lived and worked as tribes, even if many aspects of their traditional lifestyles were no longer possible. From 1924 to 1927, multi-millionaire John D. Rockefeller funded a major sociological survey of Indian tribes. The resulting 1928 Meriam Report documented the appalling poverty, disease, and maladjustment pervading many tribes. It recommended that Congress support Indian community life and land. Six years later, in 1934, Congress passed the Wheeler-Howard Act, also called the Indian Reorganization Act and the Indian New Deal. It essentially reestablished reservations, consolidating Indian land, establishing tribal governments and court systems, and supporting cultural development programs. Ironically, the reservations that had once been considered anathema to most Indians were now viewed as their salvation.

For the next decade, positive advances were made on many reservations, but following World War II, the pendulum swung once again. The Indian Claims Commission, established in 1946, worked to satisfy tribal claims against the government for such things as lands taken in violation of treaties. But the settlement of these claims, combined with documentation of Indian advances, paved the way for a new policy—reservation termination. Those who favored the policy said that Indians no longer needed the special status that reservations and the federal government afforded them. The Bureau of Indian Affairs moved to end federal programs that provided reservations with health care, education, and other support, and the government moved to end the reservation status of tribes deemed ready for self-sufficient participation in American society. At the same time, programs were put into place to encourage Indians to leave reservation lands and move to cities where they would have greater employment opportunities. Not coincidentally, this would also leave reservation land and resources available for acquisition by the government and private corporations.

Only a few tribes were actually terminated, but the results were disastrous. Indians protested their treatment, and once again the government had to look at reservations as a potentially positive force in Indian life. By 1970, government policy had returned to a plan of support for the reservations and allowing tribes to establish their own governments and determine their own futures. Tribes regained some of their lost land, and many of them learned how to do business with white culture. Twenty-five tribes whose reservations contained valuable oil and other energy resources banded together to form CERT (the Council of Energy Resource Tribes), which gave them greater negotiating power than any individual tribe could have. Others took advantage of their "exotic" status and developed booming tourist industries. Still others discovered a previously unthought of source of income—gambling. Indian casinos have become big business in some thirty states.

All this is not to say that Indian reservations in general are thriving communities today. Many continue to struggle with extraordinarily high rates of poverty, unemployment, welfare dependency, alcoholism, and suicide. And despite some success, tribes and individuals continue to struggle with the questions of what it means to be an Indian and whether it is possible to retain an Indian cultural identity while participating in the greater American culture.

The articles in this book have been collected from a variety of historical sources. They focus primarily on the relationship between the Indians and the government, but they also present the views of individuals wrestling with the issues surrounding the establishment and perpetuation of the reservation system.

Notes

1. Eric Mayer, "Land Conflicts." www.emayzine.com/lectures/indian%20land%20disputes.html.
2. William C. Canby Jr., *American Indian Law in a Nutshell.* St. Paul: West, 1981, p. 10.
3. Francis Paul Prucha, *American Indian Policy in the Formative Years: The Indian Trade and Intercourse Acts, 1790–1834.* Lincoln: University of Nebraska Press, 1962, p. 2.
4. Prucha, *American Indian Policy in the Formative Years*, p. 2.
5. Judith Nies, *Native American History: A Chronology of a Culture's Vast Achievements and Their Links to World Events.* New York: Ballantine, 1996, p. 247.
6. Quoted in Nies, *Native American History*, p. 245.
7. Quoted in Annette Rosenstiel, *Red & White: Indian Views of the White Man, 1492–1982.* New York: Universe Books, 1983, p. 134.
8. Canby, *American Indian Law in a Nutshell*, p. 13.
9. Quoted in Angie Debo, *A History of the Indians of the United States.* Norman: University of Oklahoma Press, 1984, p. 299.

Chapter 1

Indian Removal (1825–1840)

1

The Indians Must
Move West

James Monroe

The end of the Revolutionary War allowed the new Americans to concentrate their full efforts on creating new lives and building new fortunes. For the first time, many of the former Europeans had the opportunity to acquire and develop their own land among the millions of acres in the lightly populated new country. Many times the Americans desired the lands that the continent's natives had lived on, cultivated, and hunted for centuries. The Americans acquired some of this land by treaty or purchase, but sometimes the Indians were reluctant to give up their land. Many Indians believed that the land belonged to God and was to be shared communally, not owned by individuals. They were reluctant to allow people to take sole ownership of the land so that Indians could no longer fish, hunt, and farm.

Both Indians and whites initiated many conflicts as they came into contact with one another over the land issue. In some instances, whites turned to their new government to reinforce their perceived rights to the land. A major example—though far from the only one—is the state of Georgia.

Georgia had rich soil good for planting cotton and tobacco. It also had vast mineral resources, including coal and gold. But Georgia did not own all of the land within its borders. The Hopewell treaties, signed by the United States and several Southern Indian tribes in 1785-6, guaranteed a substantial land tract to the Cherokee. This land was to be governed by the Cherokee and to be free of interference from the settlers or the state. Only a short time after the treaties were signed, the government changed its mind, promising that this

James Monroe's speech to the Senate and House of Representatives, January 27, 1825.

land would be negotiated away from the Indians and returned to Georgia. As the nineteenth century moved into its second decade, Georgians became more and more anxious to get rid of the "foreign nation" in their midst and to move the Indians out.

President James Monroe agreed that the best solution to the conflicts, for both Indians and whites, was for the Indians to move to the more open country in the West. In the following speech to Congress, given on January 28, 1825, he proposes a plan to encourage the Indians to voluntarily move west. They would not be moving onto reservations as such, but the federal government would agree to set aside—reserve— certain land for them that they could govern in their own manner and that white settlers would not be allowed to infringe on.

Monroe, the fifth U.S. president (1817–1825), was active in law and politics from his early twenties, serving in various offices. While governor of Virginia (1799–1802) he also served as special envoy to France, where he had previously held another diplomatic position. During this second tenure in France, he helped enlarge the United States by acquiring New Orleans from France and Florida from Spain. He may be best remembered for the Monroe Doctrine, which he established while president. The doctrine firmly separated America's interests from Europe's. It declared that the United States would not involve itself in any European matters and expected that Europe would keep its hands off America. This policy heavily influenced America's foreign relations for many years to come.

Being deeply impressed with the opinion that the removal of the Indian tribes from the lands which they now occupy within the limits of the several States and Territories to the country lying westward and northward thereof, within our acknowledged boundaries, is of very high importance to our Union, and may be accomplished on conditions and in a manner to promote the interest and happiness of those tribes, the attention of the Government has been long drawn with great solicitude to the object. For the removal of the tribes within the limits of the State of Georgia the motive has been peculiarly strong, arising from the compact with that State whereby the United States are bound to extinguish the Indian title to the lands within it whenever it may be done peaceably and on reasonable conditions. In the fulfillment of this compact, I have thought that the United States should act with a generous spirit; that they should omit nothing which should comport with a liberal construction of the instrument and likewise be in accordance with the just rights of those tribes. From the view which I have taken of the subject I am satisfied that in the discharge of these important duties in regard to both the parties alluded to the United States will have to encounter no conflicting interests with either. On the contrary, that the removal of the tribes from the territory which they now inhabit to that which was designated in the message at the commencement of the session, which would accomplish the object for Georgia, under a well-digested plan for their government and civilization, which should be agreeable to themselves, would not only shield them from impending ruin, but promote their welfare and happiness. Experience has clearly demonstrated that in their present state it is impossible to incorporate them in such masses, in any form whatever, into our system. It has also demonstrated with equal certainty that without a timely anticipation of and provision against the dangers to which they are exposed, under causes which it will be difficult, if not impossible, to control, their degradation and extermination will be inevitable.

Honorable Removal

The great object to be accomplished is the removal of these tribes to the territory designated on conditions which shall be satisfactory to themselves and honorable to the United States. This can be done only by conveying to each tribe a good title to an adequate portion of land to which it may consent to remove, and by providing for it there a system of internal government which shall protect their property from invasion, and, by the regular progress of improvement and civilization, prevent that degeneracy which has generally marked the transition from the one to the other state.

I transmit herewith a report from the Secretary of War, which presents the best estimate which can be formed, from the documents in that Department, of the number of Indians within our States and Territories and of the amount of lands held by the several tribes within each; of the state of the country lying northward and westward thereof, within our acknowledged boundaries; of the parts to which the Indian title has already been extinguished, and of the conditions on which other parts, in an amount which may be adequate to the object contemplated, may be obtained. By this report it appears that the Indian title has already been extinguished to extensive tracts in that quarter, and that other portions may be acquired to the extent desired on very moderate conditions. Satisfied I also am that the removal proposed is not only practicable, but that the advantages attending it to the Indians may be made so apparent to them that all the tribes, even those most opposed, may be induced to accede to it at no very distant day.

The digest of such a government, with the consent of the Indians, which should be endowed with sufficient power to meet all the objects contemplated—to connect the several tribes together in a bond of amity and preserve order in each; to prevent intrusions on their property; to teach them by regular instruction the arts of civilized life and make them a civilized people—is an object of very high importance. It is the powerful consideration which we have to offer to these tribes as an inducement to relinquish the lands on which they now reside and to remove to those which are designated. It is not doubted that this arrangement will present considerations of sufficient force to surmount all their prejudices in favor of the soil of their nativity, however strong they may be. Their elders have sufficient intelligence to discern the certain progress of events in the present train, and sufficient virtue, by yielding to momentary sacrifices, to protect their families and posterity from inevitable destruction. They will also perceive that they may thus attain an elevation to which as communities they could not otherwise aspire.

A Harmonious Result

To the United States the proposed arrangement offers many important advantages in addition to those which have been already enumerated. By the establishment of such a government over these tribes with their consent we become in reality their benefactors. The relation of conflicting interests which has heretofore existed between them and our frontier settlements will cease. There will be no more wars between them and the United States. Adopting such a government, their movement will be in harmony with us, and its good effect be felt throughout the whole extent of our territory to the Pacific. It may fairly be presumed that, through the agency of such a government, the condition of all the tribes inhabiting that vast region may be essentially improved; that permanent peace may be preserved with them, and our commerce be much extended.

With a view to this important object I recommend it to Congress to adopt, by solemn declaration, certain fundamental principles in accord with those above suggested, as the basis of such arrangements as may be entered into with the several tribes, to the strict observance of which the faith of the nation shall be pledged. I recommend it also to Congress to provide by law for the appointment of a suitable number of commissioners who shall, under the direction of the President, be authorized to visit and explain to the several tribes the objects of the Government, and to make with them, according to their instructions, such arrangements as shall be best calculated to carry those objects into effect.

By the establishment of such a government over these tribes with their consent we become in reality their benefactors.

A negotiation is now depending with the Creek Nation for the cession of lands held by it within the limits of Georgia, and with a reasonable prospect of success. It is presumed, however, that the result will not be known during the present session of Congress. To give effect to this negotiation and to the negotiations which it is proposed to hold with all the other tribes within the limits of the several States and Territories on the principles and for the purposes stated, it is recommended that an adequate appropriation be now made by Congress.

2

The Indians Must Be Moved to the West

Andrew Jackson

In 1828, after many years of trying to get the Indian tribes in Georgia to give up their land, Georgia's governor signed a series of laws that progressively reduced Indians' rights in Georgia and paved the way for taking their land and forcing them to leave the state.

The Cherokee took Georgia to the Supreme Court, arguing that because of the Hopewell treaty, signed in 1785, the Cherokee were a separate nation not subject to Georgia's authority. In *Cherokee Nation v. Georgia*, concluded in 1831, the Court ruled against the Indians, stating that the Cherokee were not a separate "foreign" nation, but were instead a "domestic dependent nation." Supreme Court Justice John Marshall wrote that the Cherokee

> acknowledge themselves in their treaties to be under the protection of the United States, subject to many of those restraints which are imposed upon our own citizens. They acknowledge themselves in their treaties to be under the protection of the United States; they admit that the United States shall have the sole and exclusive rights of regulating the trade with them, and managing all their affairs as they think proper. . . .

> It may well be doubted whether those tribes which reside within the acknowledged boundaries of the United States can, with any strict accuracy, be denominated foreign nations. They may, more correctly, perhaps, be denominated domestic dependent

Andrew Jackson's Second Annual Message, given before the House of Representatives, December 6, 1830.

nations. . . . They are in a state of pupilage. Their relation to the United States resembles that of a ward to his guardian.

Samuel A. Wooster, a Christian missionary who was arrested for flouting Georgia's laws by living among the Cherokee, appealed his arrest to the Supreme Court on the basis that the Cherokee were, indeed, an independent nation. John Marshall once again wrote the Court's opinion, but this time the Court reversed its earlier decision and declared the Cherokee a nation. The Court pointed to substantial earlier actions showing that Georgia did indeed consider the Cherokee a nation. In the 1832 *Wooster v. Georgia* opinion, Marshall wrote:

Various acts of her [Georgia's] legislature have been cited in the [plaintiff's] argument . . . all tending to prove her acquiescence in the universal conviction that the Indian nations possessed a full right in the lands they occupied, until that right should be extinguished by the United States, with their consent: that their territory was separated from that of any state within whose chartered limits they might reside, by a boundary line, established by treaties: that, within their boundary, they possessed rights with which no state could interfere.

In the meantime, in 1830, Congress passed the Indian Removal Act, which stated that the government could appropriate Indian lands for any reason whatsoever, giving in exchange equivalent land in some other part of the country. In effect, Congress legislated the right of the federal government to force Indians to leave treaty-guaranteed lands and to move wherever the government wanted them to, in this instance to a newly created "Indian Territory" west of the Mississippi in what is now Kansas, Arkansas, and (especially) Oklahoma.

Andrew Jackson, the seventh President of the United States (1828–1836), was ardently in favor of Indian removal to the West. He even defied the 1832 Supreme Court *Wooster v. Georgia* ruling by sending federal troops to help Georgia forcibly remove the Indians from their land and escort them to Indian Territory.

During his time in office, Jackson made several pronouncements favoring Indian removal. In his first annual presidential message to Congress, he encouraged Congress to establish an Indian territory west of the Mississippi for Indians to move to. He declared that "this emigration should be voluntary, for it would be as cruel as unjust to compel the aborigines to abandon the graves of their fathers and seek a home in a distant land." By his second annual message to Congress, he had become much more adamant about the need for the Indians to move, voluntarily or not. The portion of his second annual message that relates to the Indians is reprinted below.

Before his presidency, Andrew Jackson was a major landholder and Indian fighter who, according to biographer Bruce E. Johansen, "had scorched the memories of Native American people for decades. . . . As a general in the U.S. Army, Jackson blazed a trail of fire throughout the South, refusing to retreat even when his superiors ordered him to relent." In one battle against the Southern tribes, his troops and the Creeks who fought with them lost about seventy men; the Cherokees they were battling lost nearly seven hundred and fifty. Jackson's ferocious fighting and aggressive treaty-making gained the U.S. huge chunks of Indian land in Florida, Alabama, and Georgia. He firmly believed that whites had the right to the lands they wanted and that Indians should move out to accommodate the whites. The treaties that had been made, he said, could be ignored because they were made by the federal government in violation of the states' rights.

During Jackson's presidency, according to Johansen, the United States acquired "more than 100 million acres of Native American land . . . in exchange for roughly $68 million (68 cents an acre) and 32 million acres west of the Mississippi River [Indian Territory], much of which was subsequently taken as well."

It gives me pleasure to announce to Congress that the benevolent policy of the Government, steadily pursued for nearly thirty years, in relation to the removal of the Indians beyond the white settlements is approaching to a happy consummation. Two important tribes have accepted the provision made for their removal at the last session of Congress, and it is believed that their example will induce the remaining tribes also to seek the same obvious advantages.

The consequences of a speedy removal will be important to the United States, to individual States, and the Indians themselves. The pecuniary advantages which it promises to the Government are the least of its recommendations. It puts an end to all possible danger of collision between the authorities of the General and State Government on account of the Indians. It will place a dense and civilized population in large tracts of country now occupied by a few savage hunters. By opening the whole territory between Tennessee on the north and Louisiana on the south to the settlement of the whites it will incalculably strengthen the southwestern frontier and render the adjacent States strong enough to repel future invasions without remote aid. It will relieve the whole State of Mississippi and the western part of Alabama of Indian occupancy, and enable those States to advance rapidly in population, wealth, and power. It will separate the Indians from immediate contact with settlements of whites; free them from the power of the States; enable them to pursue happiness in their own way and under their own rude institutions; will retard the progress of decay, which is lessening their numbers, and perhaps cause them gradually, under the protection of the Government and through the influence of good counsels, to cast off their savage habits and become an interesting, civilized, and Christian community. These consequences, some of them so certain and the rest so probable, make the complete execution of the plan sanctioned by Congress at their last session an object of much solicitude.

Toward the aborigines of the country no one can indulge a more friendly feeling than myself, or would go further in attempting to reclaim them from their wandering habits and make them a happy, prosperous people. I have endeavored to impress upon them my own solemn convictions of the duties and powers of the General Government in relation to the State authorities. For the justice of the laws passed by the States within the scope of their reserved powers they are not responsible to this Government. As individuals we may entertain and express our opinions of their acts, but as a Government we have as little right to control them as we have to prescribe laws for other nations.

Generous Offers

With a full understanding of the subject, the Choctaw and the Chickasaw tribes have with great unanimity determined to avail themselves of the liberal offers presented by the act of Congress, and have agreed to remove beyond the Mississippi River. Treaties have been made with them, which in due season will be submitted for consideration. In negotiating these treaties they were made to understand their true condition, and they preferred maintaining their independence in the Western forests to submitting to the laws of the States in which they now reside. These treaties, being probably the last which will ever be made with them, are characterized by great liberality on the part of the government. They give the Indians a liberal sum in consideration of their removal, and comfortable subsistence on their arrival at their new homes. If it be their real interest to maintain a separate existence, they will there be at liberty to do so without the inconveniences and vexations to which they would unavoidably have been subject in Alabama and Mississippi.

Humanity has often wept over the fate of the aborigines of this country, and philanthropy has been long busily employed in devising means to avert it, but its progress has never for a moment been arrested, and one by one have many powerful tribes disappeared from the earth. To follow to the tomb the last of his race and to tread on the graves of extinct nations excite melancholy reflections. But true philanthropy reconciles the mind to these vicissitudes as it does to the extinction of one generation to make room for another. In the monuments and fortresses of an unknown people, spread over the extensive regions of the West, we behold the memorials of a once powerful race, which was exterminated or has disappeared to make room for the existing savage tribes. Nor is there anything in this which, upon a comprehensive view of the general interests of the human race, is to be regretted. Philanthropy could not wish to see this continent restored to the condition in which it was found by our forefathers. What good man would prefer a country covered with forests and ranged by a few thousand savages to our extensive Republic, studded with cities, towns, and prosperous farms, embellished with all the improvements which art can devise or industry execute, occupied by more than 12,000,000 happy people, and filled with all the blessings of liberty, civilization, and religion?

Leaving the Past Behind

The present policy of the Government is but a continuation of the same progressive change by a milder process. The tribes which occupied the countries now constituting the Eastern States were annihilated or have melted away to make room for the whites. The waves of population and civilization are rolling to the westward, and we now propose to acquire the countries occupied by the red men of the South and West by a fair exchange, and, at the expense of the United States, to send them to a land where their existence may be prolonged and perhaps made perpetual. Doubtless it will be painful to leave the graves of their fathers; but what do they more than our ancestors did or than our children are now doing? To better their condition in an unknown land our forefathers left all that was dear in earthly objects. Our children by thousands yearly leave the land of their birth to seek new homes in distant regions. Does Humanity weep at these painful separations from everything, animate and inanimate, with which the young heart has become entwined? Far from it. It is rather a source of joy that our country affords scope where our young population may range unconstrained in body or in mind, developing the power and faculties of man in their highest perfection. These remove hundreds and almost thousands of miles at their own expense, purchase his lands, to give him a new and extensive territory, to pay the expense of his removal, and support him a year in his new abode? How many thousands of our own people would gladly embrace the opportunity of removing to the West on such conditions! If the offers made to the Indians were extended to them, they would be hailed with gratitude and joy.

And is it supposed that the wandering savage has a stronger attachment to his home than the settled, civilized Christian? Is it more afflicting to him to leave the graves of his fathers than it is to our brothers and children? Rightly considered, the policy of the General Government toward the red man is not only liberal, but generous. He is unwilling to submit to the laws of the States and mingle with their population. To save him from this alternative, or perhaps utter annihilation, the General Government kindly offers him a new home, and proposes to pay the whole expense of his removal and settlement.

The Power of the States

In the consummation of a policy originating at an early period, and steadily pursued by every Administration within

the present century—so just to the States and so generous
to the Indians—the Executive feels it has a right to expect
the cooperation of Congress and of all good and disinter-
ested men. The States, moreover, have a right to demand it.
It was substantially a part of the compact which made them
members of our Confederacy. With Georgia there is an express contract; with the new States an implied one of equal
obligation. Why, in authorizing Ohio, Indiana, Illinois,
Missouri, Mississippi, and Alabama to form constitutions
and become separate States, did Congress include within
their limits extensive tracts of Indian lands, and, in some instances, powerful Indian tribes? Was it not understood by
both parties that the power of the States was to be coexten-
sive with their limits, and that with all convenient dispatch
the General Government should extinguish the Indian title
and remove every obstruction to the complete jurisdiction
of the State governments over the soil? Probably not one of
those States would have accepted a separate existence—certainly it would never have been granted by Congress—had
it been understood that they were to be confined forever to
those small portions of their nominal territory the Indian
title to which had at the time been extinguished.

---

*It is . . . a duty which this government owes to
the new States to extinguish as soon as possible
the Indian title to all lands . . . included within
their [the state's] limits.*

It is, therefore, a duty which this Government owes to
the new States to extinguish as soon as possible the Indian
title to all lands which Congress themselves have included
within their limits. When this is done the duties of the General Government in relation to the States and the Indians
within their limits are at an end. The Indians may leave the
State or not, as they choose. The purchase of their lands
does not alter in the least their personal relations with the
State government. No act of the General Government has
ever been deemed necessary to give the States jurisdiction
over the persons of the Indians. That they possess by virtue
of their own sovereign power within their own limits in as
full a manner before as after the purchase of the Indian

lands; nor can this Government add to or diminish it.

May we not hope, therefore, that all good citizens, and none more zealously than those who think the Indians oppressed by subjection to the laws of the States, will unite in attempting to open the eyes of those children of the forest to their true condition, and by a speedy removal to relieve them from all the evils, real or imaginary, present or prospective, with which they may be supposed to be threatened.

3

Indian Removal
Is a Disgrace

Ralph Waldo Emerson

Not all Americans were in favor of forcing the Indians to leave their lands. Some people felt empathy for the Indians, while others objected to the legal inconsistency in the treaties made and broken.

On April 23, 1838, Ralph Waldo Emerson, a young poet, essayist, philosopher, and leader of a prominent intellectual movement called Transcendentalism, wrote the letter below. He addressed it to President Martin van Buren but actually sent it to an acquaintance, Massachusetts Congressman John Reed, who arranged for it to be published in newspapers. As happens today, each newspaper edits letters to its own standards. In the version of the letter published in the *Washington Intelligencer*, reprinted below, Emerson states that he and other Americans feel deep outrage at the impending Cherokee Removal.

Ralph Waldo Emerson became one of the preeminent writers, philosophers, and lecturers of the nineteenth century. His Transcendentalist movement went against the empiricist grain of the time, favoring intuition, not reason, as the guide to truth.

Sir: The seat you fill places you in a relation of credit and nearness to every citizen. By right and natural position, every citizen is your friend. Before any acts contrary to his own judgement or interest have repelled the affections of any man, each may look with trust and living anticipation to your government. Each has the highest right to call your attention to such subjects as are of a public nature, and

Ralph Waldo Emerson, "Letter to President Van Buren," 1838.

properly belong to the chief magistrate; and the chief magistrate will feel a joy in meeting such confidence. In this belief and at the instance of a few of my friends and neighbors, I crave of your patience a short hearing for their sentiments and my own: and the circumstance that my name will be utterly unknown to you will only give the fairer chance to your equitable construction of what I have to say.

Sir, my communication respects the sinister rumors that fill this part of the country concerning the Cherokee people. The interest always felt in the aboriginal population—an interest naturally growing as that decays—has been heightened in regard to this tribe. Even in our distant State some good rumor of their worth and civility has arrived. We have learned with joy their improvement in the social arts. We have read their newspapers. We have seen some of them in our schools and colleges. In common with the great body of the American people, we have witnessed with sympathy the painful labors of these red men to redeem their own race from the doom of eternal inferiority, and to borrow and domesticate in the tribe the arts and customs of the Caucasian race. And notwithstanding the unaccountable apathy with which of late years the Indians have been sometimes abandoned to their enemies, it is not to be doubted that it is the good pleasure and the understanding of all humane persons in the Republic, of the men and the matrons sitting in the thriving independent families all over the land, that they shall be duly cared for; that they shall taste justice and love from all to whom we have delegated the office of dealing with them.

Not the Nation's Will

The newspapers now inform us that, in December, 1835, a treaty contracting for the exchange of all the Cherokee territory was pretended to be made by an agent on the part of the United States with some persons appearing on the part of the Cherokees; that the fact afterwards transpired that these deputies did by no means represent the will of the nation; and that, out of eighteen thousand souls composing the nation, fifteen thousand six hundred and sixty-eight have protested against the so-called treaty. It now appears that the government of the United States choose to hold the Cherokees to this sham treaty, and are proceeding to execute the same. Almost the entire Cherokee Nation stand up and say, "This is not our act. Behold us. Here we are. Do not mistake that handful of deserters for us"; and the American President and the Cabinet, the Senate and the House of Representatives, neither hear these men nor see them, and are contracting to put this active nation into carts and boats, and to drag them over mountains and rivers to a wilderness at a vast distance beyond the Mississippi. And a paper purporting to be an army order fixes a month from this day as the hour for this doleful removal.

In the name of God, sir, we ask you if this be so. Do the newspapers rightly inform us? Men and women with pale and perplexed faces meet one another in the streets and churches here, and ask if this be so. We have inquired if this be a gross misrepresentation from the party opposed to the government and anxious to blacken it with the people. We have looked at the newspapers of different parties and find a horrid confirmation of the tale. We are slow to believe it. We hoped the Indians were misinformed, and that their remonstrance was premature, and will turn out to be a needless act of terror.

The piety, the principle that is left in the United States, if only in its coarsest form, a regard to the speech of men, forbid us to entertain it as a fact. Such a dereliction of all faith and virtue, such a denial of justice, and such deafness to screams for mercy were never heard of in times of peace and in the dealing of a nation with its own allies and wards, since the earth was made. Sir, does this government think that the people of the United States are become savage and mad? From their mind are the sentiments of love and a good nature wiped clean out? The soul of man, the justice, the mercy that is the heart's heart in all men, from Maine to Georgia, does abhor this business.

In speaking thus the sentiments of my neighbors and my own, perhaps I overstep the bounds of decorum. But would it not be a higher indecorum coldly to argue a matter like this? We only state the fact that a crime is projected that confounds our understandings by its magnitude, a crime that really deprives us as well as the Cherokees of a country for how could we call the conspiracy that should crush these poor Indians our government, or the land that was cursed by their parting and dying imprecations our country, any more? You, sir, will bring down that renowned chair in which you sit into infamy if your seal is set to this instrument of perfidy; and the name of this nation, hitherto the sweet omen of religion and liberty, will stink to the world.

Shall Justice Be Done?

You will not do us the injustice of connecting this remonstrance with any sectional and party feeling. It is in our hearts the simplest commandment of brotherly love. We will not have this great and solemn claim upon national and human justice huddled aside under the flimsy plea of its being a party act. Sir, to us the questions upon which the government and the people have been agitating during the past year, touching the prostration of the currency and of trade, seem but motes in comparison. These hard times, it is true, have brought the discussion home to every farmhouse and poor man's house in this town; but it is the chirping of grasshoppers beside the immortal question whether justice shall be done by the race civilized to the race of savage man, whether all the attributes of reason, of civility, of justice, and even of mercy, shall be put off by the American people, and so vast an outrage upon the Cherokee Nation and upon human nature shall be consummated.

One circumstance lessens the reluctance with which I intrude at this time on your attention my conviction that the government ought to be admonished of a new historical fact, which the discussion of this question has disclosed, namely, that there exists in a great part of the Northern people a gloomy diffidence in the *moral* character of the government.

The soul of man, the justice, the mercy that is the heart's heart in all men, from Maine to Georgia, does abhor this business.

On the broaching of this question, a general expression of despondency, of disbelief that any good will accrue from a remonstrance on an act of fraud and robbery, appeared in those men to whom we naturally turn for aid and counsel. Will the American government steal? Will it lie? Will it kill?—We ask triumphantly. Our counselors and old statesmen here say that ten years ago they would have staked their lives on the affirmation that the proposed Indian measures could not be executed; that the unanimous country would put them down. And now the steps of this crime follow each other so fast, at such fatally quick time, that the millions of virtuous citizens, whose agents the government are, have no place to interpose, and must shut their eyes until the last howl and wailing of these tormented villages and tribes shall afflict the ear of the world.

I will not hide from you, as an indication of the alarming distrust, that a letter addressed as mine is, and suggesting to the mind of the Executive the plain obligations of man, has a burlesque character in the apprehensions of some of my friends. I, sir, will not beforehand treat you with the contumely of this distrust. I will at least state to you this fact, and show you how plain and humane people, whose love would be honor, regard the policy of the government, and what injurious inferences they draw as to the minds of the governors. A man with your experience in affairs must have seen cause to appreciate the futility of opposition to the moral sentiment. However feeble the sufferer and however great the oppressor, it is in the nature of things that the blow should recoil upon the aggressor. For God is in the sentiment, and it cannot be withstood. The potentate and the people perish before it; but with it, and its executor, they are omnipotent.

I write thus, sir, to inform you of the state of mind these Indian tidings have awakened here, and to pray with one voice more that you, whose hands are strong with the delegated power of fifteen millions of men, will avert with that might the terrific injury which threatens the Cherokee tribe.

With great respect, sir, I am your fellow citizen,
RALPH WALDO EMERSON

4
A Tragic Journey

John G. Burnett

In 1838, despite the long days in court and the pleas that had been made to the president, the forced Cherokee removal began. Contravening the Supreme Court's ruling, President Jackson authorized federal troops to help Georgia in its effort. Seven thousand federal troops helped the Georgian soldiers round up some 16,000 Cherokee, whites married to Cherokee, and others with Cherokee blood. The people set off on the six-month trek from Georgia to Oklahoma. James Mooney, an anthropologist who spent his career living among and studying the Indians, reported,

> Under [General Winfield] Scott's orders the troops were disposed at various points throughout the Cherokee country, where stockade forts were erected for gathering in and holding the Indians preparatory to removal. From these, squads of troops were sent to search out with rifle and bayonet every small cabin hidden away in the coves or by the sides of the mountain streams, to seize and bring in as prisoners all the occupants, however or wherever they might be found. Families at dinner were startled by the sudden gleam of bayonets in the doorway and rose up to be driven with blows and oaths along the weary miles of trail that led to the stockade. Men were seized in their fields or going along the road, women were taken from their [spinning] wheels and children from their play. In many cases, on turning for one last look as they crossed the ridge, they saw their homes in flames, fired by the lawless rabble that followed on the heels of the soldiers to loot and pillage.

John G. Burnett, "The Cherokee Removal Through the Eyes of a Private Soldier," December 11, 1890. Reprinted courtesy of The Museum of the Cherokee Indian.

Mooney wrote that in early June 1838, "when nearly seventeen thousand Cherokee had thus been gathered into the various stockades, the work of removal began." Heat and sickness overwhelmed the Indians, and they petitioned General Scott to delay the journey until fall, when they would leave Georgia voluntarily. Scott agreed, on condition that all would have left by October 30. In October, the journey began in earnest. "It was like the march of an army, regiment after regiment, the [supply] wagons in the center, the officers along the line and the horsemen on the flanks and at the rear," Mooney wrote.

Of course, those riding were, for the most part, soldiers. Most Indians had no transportation other than their own feet. Parents carried small children. Farm animals and most personal goods had to be left behind. And unfortunately, delaying the journey didn't lessen the trip's difficulty. Soon, rain, ice, snow, and winds beat the people as savagely as had the summer sun. Sickness and death were rampant. Nearly one-fourth of the Cherokee died on the "trail of tears," as it has come to be called.

The Cherokee Removal was not the only time Indian tribes were relocated. Between 1816 and 1850 more than 100,000 Indians from all parts of the country were relocated to Indian Territory or other lands west of the Mississippi. Lesser numbers were moved both before and after that time. Some tribes were moved again and again.

Not all of those ordered to help in the Cherokee Removal were enthusiastic about their job. John G. Burnett, author of the article below, was a young army private assigned to accompany the Indians on their long, heart-breaking journey. Burnett had spent much of his youth in the friendly company of Indians, so he was particularly saddened by the task he had been assigned. The article below is a letter he wrote to his grandchildren more than 50 years after the long march. In it, he recalls what he describes as a murderous journey.

The Cherokee were one of a group of southern tribes known as the Five Civilized Tribes (Cherokee, Chickasaw, Choctaw, Creek, and Seminole), called that because they lived similarly to whites in many respects. They had a formal constitution, stable agricultural lives, schools, and even slaves. Georgia wanted them out of the state for several reasons, but they boiled down to perhaps three main ones: Georgia's sovereignty (the state did not want an independent nation within its borders), land greed, and gold (in 1829, gold was discovered on Cherokee lands).

The place designated for Cherokee relocation was called Indian Territory. It was located west of the Mississippi in what is primarily today's Oklahoma. People from many different tribes were relocated there, people as different from one another in language and customs as citizens from many different nations.

Many historians consider this the true beginning of the reservation system. The Indians were essentially confined to a particular area of land—land that the government did not anticipate white settlers would ever want, as it was mostly hot, barren desert. The land was "reserved" for them, thus the term "reservation." Unlike the reservation system that was established a few years later, the early tribes in Indian Territory were allowed to set up their own governing systems, but after a time, they were subject once again to federal regulation and the invasion of whites looking for ever more land to settle and exploit.

This is my birthday December the 11th 1890, I am eighty years old today. I was born at Kings Iron Works in Sullivan County, Tennessee, December the 11th, 1810. I grew into manhood fishing in Beaver Creek and roaming through the forest hunting the Deer the wild Boar and the timber Wolf. Often spending weeks at a time in the solitary wilderness with no companions but my rifle, hunting knife, and a small hatchet that I carried in my belt in all of my wilderness wanderings.

On these long hunting trips I met and became acquainted with many of the Cherokee Indians, hunting with them by day and sleeping around their camp fires by night. I learned to speak their language, and they taught me the arts of trailing and building traps and snares. On one of my long hunts in the fall of 1829 I found a young Cherokee who had been shot by a roving band of hunters and who had eluded his pursuers and concealed himself under a shelving rock. Weak from loss of blood the poor creature was unable to walk and almost famished for water. I carried him to a spring bathed and bandaged the bullet wound, built a shelter out of bark peeled from a dead chestnut tree, nursed and protected him feeding him on chestnuts and roasted deer meat. When he was able to travel I accompanied him to the home of his people and remained so long that I was given up for lost. By this time I had become an expert rifleman and fairly good archer and a good trapper and spent most of my time in the forest in quest of game.

The Removal Begins

The removal of the Cherokee Indians from their life long homes in the year of 1838 found me a young man in the prime of life and a Private soldier in the American Army. Being acquainted with many of the Indians and able to fluently speak their language, I was sent as interpreter into the Smoky Mountain Country in May, 1838, and witnessed the execution of the most brutal order in the History of American Warfare. I saw the helpless Cherokees arrested and dragged from their homes, and driven at the bayonet point into the stockades. And in the chill of a drizzling rain on an October morning I saw them loaded like cattle or sheep into six hundred and forty-five wagons and started toward the west.

One can never forget the sadness and solemnity of that morning. Chief John Ross led in prayer and when the bugle sounded and the wagons started rolling many of the children rose to their feet and waved their little hands good-by to their mountain homes, knowing they were leaving them forever. Many of these helpless people did not have blankets and many of them had been driven from home barefooted.

Trail of Death

On the morning of November the 17th we encountered a terrific sleet and snow storm with freezing temperatures and from that day until we reached the end of the fateful journey on March the 26th 1839, the sufferings of the Cherokees were awful. The trail of the exiles was a trail of death. They had to sleep in the wagons and on the ground without fire. And I have known as many as twenty-two of them to die in one night of pneumonia due to ill treatment, cold, and exposure. Among this number was the beautiful Christian wife of Chief John Ross. This noble hearted woman died a martyr to childhood, giving her only blanket for the protection of a sick child. She rode thinly clad through a blinding sleet and snow storm, developed pneumonia and died in the still hours of a bleak winter night, with her head resting on Lieutenant Gregg's saddle blanket.

I made the long journey to the west with the Cherokees and did all that a Private soldier could do to alleviate their sufferings. When on guard duty at night I have many times walked my beat in my blouse in order that some sick child might have the warmth of my overcoat.

I was on guard duty the night Mrs. Ross died. When relieved at midnight I did not retire, but remained around the wagon out of sympathy for Chief Ross, and at daylight was detailed by Captain McClellan to assist in the burial like the other unfortunates who died on the way. Her uncoffined body was buried in a shallow grave by the roadside far from her native mountain home, and the sorrowing Cavalcade moved on. . . .

Gold Sealed the Cherokees' Doom

The long painful journey to the west ended March 26th, 1839, with four-thousand silent graves reaching from the foothills of the Smoky Mountains to what is known as the Indian territory in the West. And covetousness on the part of the white race was the cause of all that the Cherokees had to suffer.

Ever since Ferdinand DeSoto made his journey through the Indian country in the year of 1540, there had been a tradition of a rich Gold mine somewhere in the Smoky Mountain Country, and I think the tradition was true. At a festival at Echata on Christmas night 1829, I danced and played with Indian girls who were wearing ornaments around their necks that looked Gold.

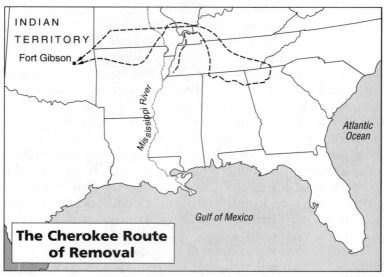

INDIAN TERRITORY

Fort Gibson

Mississippi River

Atlantic Ocean

Gulf of Mexico

The Cherokee Route of Removal

In the year of 1828, a little Indian boy living on Ward creek had sold a Gold nugget to a white trader, and that nugget sealed the doom of the Cherokees. In a short time the country was over run with armed brigands claiming to be Government Agents, who paid no attention to the rights of the Indians who were the legal possessors of the country. Crimes were committed that were a disgrace to civilization. Men were shot in cold blood, lands were confiscated. Homes were burned and the inhabitants driven out by these Gold hungry brigands.

A Cold and Indifferent President

Chief Junaluska was personally acquainted with President Andrew Jackson. Junaluska had taken five hundred of the flower of his Cherokee scouts and helped Jackson to win the battle of the Horse Shoe leaving thirty-three of them dead on the field. And in that battle Junaluska had drove his Tomahawk through the skull of a Creek warrior, when the Creek had Jackson at mercy.

Chief John Ross sent Junaluska as an envoy to plead with President Jackson for protection for his people, but Jackson's manner was cold and indifferent toward the rugged son of the forest who had saved his life. He met Junaluska, heard his plea but curtly said "Sir your audience is ended, there is nothing I can do for you." The doom of the Cherokee was sealed, Washington, D.C. had decreed that they must be driven West, and their lands given to the white man, and in May 1838 an Army of four thousand regulars, and three thousand volunteer soldiers under command of General Winfield Scott, marched into the Indian country and wrote the blackest chapter on the pages of American History.

Men working in the fields were arrested and driven to the stockades. Women were dragged from their homes by soldiers whose language they could not understand. Children were often separated from their parents and driven into the stockades with the sky for a blanket and the earth for a pillow. And often the old and infirm were prodded with bayonets to hasten them to the stockades.

In one home death had come during the night, a little sad faced child had died and was lying on a bear skin couch and some women were preparing the little body for burial. All were arrested and driven out leaving the child in the cabin. I don't know who buried the body.

In another home was a frail Mother, apparently a widow and three small children, one just a baby. When told that she must go the Mother gathered the children at her feet, prayed an humble prayer in her native tongue, patted the old family dog on the head, told the faithful creature good-by, with a baby strapped on her back and leading a child with each hand started on her exile. But the task was too great for that frail Mother. A stroke of heart failure relieved her sufferings. She sunk and died with her baby on her back, and her other two children clinging to her hands.

Murder is murder and somebody must answer, somebody must explain the streams of blood that flowed in the Indian country in the summer of 1838.

Chief Junaluska, who had saved President Jackson's life at the battle of Horse Shoe witnessed this scene, the tears gushing down his cheeks and lifting his cap he turned his face toward the Heavens and said "Oh my God if I had known at the battle of the Horse Shoe what I know now American History would have been differently written."

Crime Against a Helpless Race

At this time 1890 we are too near the removal of the Cherokees for our young people to fully understand the enormity of the crime that was committed against a helpless race, truth is the facts are being concealed from the young people of today. School children of today do not know that we are living on lands that were taken from a helpless race at the bayonet point to satisfy the white man's greed for gold.

Future generations will read and condemn the act and I do hope posterity will remember the private soldiers like myself, and like the four Cherokees who were forced by General Scott, to shoot an Indian Chief and his children had to execute the orders of our superiors. We had no choice in the matter. . . .

Murder Is Murder

However murder is murder whether committed by the villain skulking in the dark or by uniformed men stepping to the strains of martial music.

Murder is murder and somebody must answer, somebody must explain the streams of blood that flowed in the Indian country in the summer of 1838. Somebody must explain the four-thousand silent graves that mark the trail of the Cherokees to their exile. I wish I could forget it all, but the picture of six-hundred and forty-five wagons lumbering over the frozen ground with their Cargo of suffering humanity still lingers in my memory.

Let the Historian of a future day tell the sad story with its sighs, its tears and dying groans. Let the great judge of all the earth weigh our actions and reward us according to our work.

Children—Thus ends my promised birthday story. This December the 11th 1890.

Chapter 2

Reservation and Resistance (1825–1880s)

1

Change Reservation Policy to Make the Indians Independent

Charles E. Mix

From the beginning of colonial government, the colonists established a formal means of dealing with the Indians. In 1786, the Ordinance for the Regulation of Indian Affairs established two distinct Indian districts in the new republic—a Southern District and a Northern district, comprising all the Indians living, respectively, south and north of the Ohio River. A superintendent appointed for each district was in charge primarily of regulating trade issues between the settlers and the Indians. Informally assigned Indian agents helped in these matters.

In 1818, Congress formally established the position of Indian agent, a role filled at various times by military men, private citizens, and, in the latter part of the nineteenth century, representatives of missionary organizations.

Charles E. Mix, Commissioner of Indian Affairs in 1858, felt that the reservation policy being followed at the time was not only not working, but actually hampered the efforts of the Indian commissioner to do his job of facilitating Indian assimilation into white society. In the following excerpt from an official report, Mix argued that the reservations' impermanence, excessive size, and inefficiently controlled funds contributed to the Indians' disinterest in, and feeling of disconnection from, white civilization.

Charles E. Mix, "Report of the Commissioner of Indian Affairs," Senate Executive Document no. 1, 35th Cong., 2nd sess., serial 974, pp. 354–59, November 6, 1858.

From the commencement of the settlement of this country, the principle has been recognised and acted on, that the Indian tribes possessed the occupant or usufruct right to the lands they occupied, and that they were entitled to the peaceful enjoyment of that right until they were fairly and justly divested of it. Hence the numerous treaties with the various tribes, by which, for a stipulated consideration their lands have, from time to time, been acquired, as our population increased.

Fatal Errors

Experience has demonstrated that at least three serious, and, to the Indians, fatal errors have, from the beginning, marked our policy towards them, viz: their removal from place to place as our population advanced; the assignment to them of too great an extent of country, to be held in common; and the allowance of large sums of money, as annuities, for the lands ceded by them. These errors, far more than the want of capacity on the part of the Indian, have been the cause of the very limited success of our constant efforts to domesticate and civilize him. By their frequent changes of position and the possession of large bodies of land in common, they have been kept in an unsettled condition and prevented from acquiring a knowledge of separate and individual property, while their large annuities, upon which they have relied for a support, have not only tended to foster habits of indolence and profligacy, but constantly made them the victims of the lawless and inhuman sharper and speculator. The very material and marked difference between the northern Indians and those of the principal southern tribes, may be accounted for by the simple fact that the latter were permitted, for long periods, to remain undisturbed in their original locations; where, surrounded by, or in close proximity with a white population, they, to a considerable extent, acquired settled habits and a knowledge of and taste for civilized occupations and pursuits. Our present policy, as you are aware, is entirely the reverse of that heretofore pursued in the three particulars mentioned. It is to permanently locate the different tribes on reservations embracing only sufficient land for their actual occupancy; to divide this among them in severalty, and require them to live upon and cultivate the tracts assigned to them; and in lieu of money annuities, to furnish them with stock animals, agricultural implements, mechanic-shops, tools and materials, and manual labor schools for the industrial and mental education of their youth. Most of the older treaties, however, provide for annuities in money, and the department has, therefore, no authority to commute them even in cases where the Indians may desire, or could be influenced to agree to such a change. In view of this fact, and the better to enable the department to carry out its present and really more benevolent policy, I would respectfully recommend and urge that a law be enacted by Congress, empowering and requiring the department, in all cases where money annuities are provided for by existing treaties, and the assent of the Indians can be obtained, to commute them for objects and purposes of a beneficial character.

The principle of recognising and respecting the usufruct right of the Indians to the lands occupied by them, has not been so strictly adhered to in the case of the tribes in the Territories of Oregon and Washington. When a territorial government was first provided for Oregon, which then embraced the present Territory of Washington, strong inducements were held out to our people to emigrate and settle there, without the usual arrangements being made, in advance, for the extinguishment of the title of the Indians who occupied and claimed the lands. Intruded upon, ousted of their homes and possessions without any compensation, and deprived, in most cases, of their accustomed means of support, without any arrangement having been made to enable them to establish and maintain themselves in other locations, it is not a matter of surprise that they have committed many depredations upon our citizens, and been exasperated to frequent acts of hostility.

Properly Extinguishing Indian Land Rights

The Indians in Oregon and Washington number about 42,000, and are divided into 35 tribes and bands. The only treaties in force with any of them, are with those who inhabited the valuable sections of country embraced in the Rogue river, Umpqua and Willamette valleys. After repeated acts of hostility and continued depredations upon the white settlers, the Indians in Oregon were removed to, and are now living upon the reservations, one on the western and the other on the eastern side of the coast range of mountains; and the country to which their title was extinguished has rapidly filled up with an enterprising and thrifty population. In the year 1855, treaties were also entered into by the superintendent of Indian affairs for Oregon, and by Governor Stevens, *ex officio* superintendent for Washington Territory, with various other tribes and bands, for the purpose of extinguishing their title to large tracts of country, which were needed for the extension of our settlements, and to provide homes for the Indians in other and more suitable locations, where they could be controlled and domesticated. These treaties not having been ratified, the Indians were sorely disappointed in consequence of the expectations they were led to entertain of benefits and advantages to be derived from them not being realized. Moreover, the whites have gone on to occupy their country without regard to their rights, which has led the Indians to believe that they were to be dispossessed of it without compensation or any provision being made for them. This state of things has naturally had a tendency to exasperate them; and, in the opinion of well informed persons, has been the cause of their recent acts of hostility. The belief is confidently entertained, that, had the treaties referred to been ratified and put in course of execution, the difficulties that have occurred would not have taken place; and there can be but little if any doubt, that the cost of the military operations to subdue the Indians, and the losses sustained by our citizens from their depredations and hostilities, will amount to a far greater sum than would have been required to extinguish their title and establish and maintain them, for the necessary period, on properly selected reservations, had that policy in respect to them been sanctioned and timely measures taken to carry it out.

It cannot be expected that Indians situated like those in Oregon and Washington, occupying extensive sections of country, where, from the game and otherwise, they derive a comfortable support, will quietly and peaceably submit, without any equivalent, to be deprived of their homes and possessions, and to be driven off to some other locality where they cannot find their usual means of subsistence. Such a proceeding is not only contrary to our policy hitherto, but is repugnant alike to the dictates of humanity and the principles of natural justice. In all cases where the necessities of our rapidly increasing population have compelled us to displace the Indian, we have ever regarded it as a sacred and binding obligation to provide him with a home elsewhere, and to contribute liberally to his support until he could re-establish and maintain himself in his new place of residence. The policy, it is true, has been a costly one, but we have been amply repaid its expense by the revenue obtained from the sale of the lands acquired from the Indians, and by the rapid extension of our settlements and the corresponding increase in the resources and prosperity of our country.

More Superintendents Will Aid Indian Management

One of the difficulties attending the management of Indian affairs in Oregon and Washington, is the insufficiency of one superintendent for the great extent of country, and the numerous tribes and large number of Indians in the two territories. The superintendent reiterates his former representations respecting the necessity for two additional superintendencies, and your attention is respectfully recalled to the subject, as presented in the report from this office on the 6th of May last.

The superintendent again represents the necessity for the employment of a small war steamer for the protection of our settlements and the friendly Indians along Puget's Sound and the waters of Admiralty Inlet, from the hostile and predatory visits of the warlike Indians from Vancouver's Island and the neighboring British and Russian possessions, who move so swiftly in their large boats, that it is impossible to overtake or cut them off except by means of such a vessel.

California Reservations

The policy of concentrating the Indians on small reservations of land, and of sustaining them there for a limited period, until they can be induced to make the necessary exertions to support themselves, was commenced in 1853, with those in California. It is, in fact, the only course compatible with the obligations of justice and humanity, left to be pursued in regard to all those with which our advancing settlements render new and permanent arrangements necessary. We have no longer distant and extensive sections of country which we can assign them, abounding in game, from which they could derive a ready and comfortable support; a resource which has, in a great measure, failed them where they are, and in consequence of which they must, at times, be subjected to the pangs of hunger, if not actual starvation, or obtain a subsistence by depredations upon our frontier settlements. If it were practicable to prevent such depredations, the alternative to providing for the Indians in the manner indicated, would be to leave them to starve; but as it is impossible, in consequence of the very great extent of our frontier, and our limited military force, to adequately guard against such occurrences, the only alternative, in fact, to making such provision for them, is to exterminate them.

The policy of concentrating the Indians on small reservations of land . . . is . . . the only course compatible with the obligations of justice and humanity.

Five reservations have been established in California, on which, according to the reports of the agents, 11,239 Indians have been located; two in Oregon, with 3,200 Indians; and two in Texas, with 1,483. The whole amount expended in carrying out this system, thus far, has been $1,173,000 in California, and $301,833, 73 [sic] in Texas. The exact sum which has been expended on account of the reservations in Oregon has not yet been ascertained, but the whole amount disbursed for Indian purposes in that, and the territory of Washington since 1852, up to the 1st of July last, is $1,323,000. The amount disbursed in New Mexico, for the same period and purpose, $212,506, and in Utah, from 1853 to the 1st of July last, $172,000.

Reservation System Is Experimental

The operations thus far, in carrying out the reservation system, can properly be regarded as only experimental. Time and experience were required to develop any defects connected with it, and to demonstrate the proper remedies therefor. From a careful examination of the subject, and the best information in the possession of the department in regard to it, I am satisfied that serious errors have been committed; that a much larger amount has been expended than was necessary, and with but limited and insufficient results.

From what is stated by the superintendent for Oregon and Washington, in his annual report herewith, in regard to the two reservations in Oregon, it is apprehended that a great mistake was made in their location, the lands not appearing to be such as will afford the Indians a comfortable support by their cultivation, and that, consequently, so long as they are kept there they must be entirely sustained, at an enormous expense, by the government.

From accompanying reports, it would seem that in California a greater number of reservations have been established and a much heavier expense incurred than the condition and circumstances of the Indians required, as has probably been the case in respect of all the reservations or Indian colonies that have been commenced. In the outset it was the confident expectation that the heavy expense attending these colonies would rapidly diminish, from year to year, and that, after the third year at furthest, they would require but little if any outlay on the part of the government, the Indians in the meantime being taught to support themselves by their own exertions. This expectation has not been realized; neither have the expenses been diminished nor the Indians been materially improved. The fault has not, however, it is believed, been in the system, but in the manner in which it has been carried out. Too many persons have been employed to control, assist, and work for the Indians, and too much has been done for them in other respects. They have not been sufficiently thrown upon their own resources, and hence the colonies have not become any more competent to sustain themselves than they were when they first commenced. Time and experience having developed errors in the administration, of the system, the proper reforms are now being introduced.

Good Lands Will Enable Indians to Support Themselves

No more reservations should be established than are absolutely necessary for such Indians as have been, or it may be necessary to displace, in consequence of the extension of our settlements, and whose resources have thereby been cut off or so diminished that they cannot sustain themselves in their accustomed manner. Great care should be taken in the selection of the reservations, so as to isolate the Indians for a time from contact and interference from the whites. They should embrace good lands, which will well repay the efforts to cultivate them. No white persons should be suffered to go upon the reservations, and after the first year the lands should be divided and assigned to the Indians in severalty, every one being required to remain on his own tract and to cultivate it, no persons being employed for them except the requisite mechanics to keep their tools and implements in repair, and such as may be necessary, for a time, to teach them how to conduct their agricultural operations and to take care of their stock. They should also have the advantage of well conducted manual labor schools for the education of their youth in letters, habits of industry, and a knowledge of agriculture and the simpler mechanic arts. By the adoption of this course, it is believed that the colonies can very soon be made to sustain themselves, or so nearly so that the government will be subjected to but a comparatively trifling annual expense on account of them. But it is essential to the success of the system that there should be sufficient military force in the vicinity of the reservations to prevent the intrusion of improper persons upon them, to afford protection to the agents, and to aid in controlling the Indians and keeping them within the limits assigned to them.

No more reservations should be established than are absolutely necessary for such Indians as have been, or it may be necessary to displace.

It would materially aid the department in its efforts to carry out the system successfully, in respect to the Indians in California, if that State would, like Texas, so far relinquish to the general government her jurisdiction over the reservations to be permanently retained there, as to admit of the trade and intercourse laws being put in force within their limits, so as to secure the Indians against improper interference and intercourse, and to prevent the traffic with them in ardent spirits. Much good could also probably be accomplished by the introduction of a judicious system of apprenticeship, by which the orphans and other children of both sexes, could be bound out for a term of years, to upright and humane persons, to be taught suitable trades and occupations: provided the necessary State laws were enacted to authorize and regulate such a system. I would suggest the propriety of an application being made to the proper authorities of California for the requisite State legislation on both these subjects.

2

The Reservation System Has Harmed the Indians

Barboncito

The Great Peace Commission of 1867–1868 was authorized by Congress in July 1867. The Commission traveled to parts of the country where Indians and whites were in active conflict and attempted to make treaties that would end the Indian Wars—the conflicts between tribes and between tribes and whites. Congress hoped the Commission's efforts would result in safe passage for westward-bound white settlers passing through Indian lands. It also hoped to reduce the country's expenditures on Indian matters, including both the costs of military containment of the Indians and the costs of subsidizing reservations.

Most treaties that included the Indians' agreement to live on a reservation also included government subsidies for the Indians. The relocation to reservations had cost Indians their normal means of livelihood, whether it be nomadic hunting and gathering or raising food on established plots of land. In compensation, the government agreed to furnish certain kinds of supplies for a period of time while the Indians re-established themselves on the new land. Some of the difficulties the Indians faced stemmed from the inadequacy of government support or problems with its administration, and some stemmed from the "foreignness" of the lands the Indians had been removed to.

During the course of the Great Peace Commission and other, similar peace commissions that took place in the 1860s, the commissioners met with Indian tribes, listened to what they had to say, and attempted to negotiate new treaties. Many treaties were signed, although most eventually were broken by one or both sides, more often by whites.

Barboncito, in proceedings of a council with the Navajo Nation, May 28, 1868, Bosque Redondo, New Mexico Territory.

The following article is one Navajo medicine man and war leader's remarks to the Great Peace Commission when it met at Bosque Redondo, in New Mexico territory. The article was edited for style for inclusion in *Proceedings of the Great Peace Commission of 1867–1868*, edited by Vine Deloria Jr. and Raymond De Mallie. The Navajos, a sheepherding, weaving, and agricultural tribe originally from the northern part of the country, had become incensed in 1851 when the government built Fort Defiance on the Navajo reservation in Arizona, territory that treaties had reserved for Navajo use alone without interference from whites. The Indians charged that the army was using Navajo grazing land and water for its livestock. In 1858, Manuelito, a Navajo leader who found 60 of his livestock shot by soldiers, confronted the fort's officers. In retaliation, the troops destroyed Manuelito's land. Manuelito gathered more than 1,000 warriors and attacked the fort, leading to the American army's "total war" policy against the Navajos, ultimately forcing them on a 350-mile trek to Bosque Redondo, near Fort Sumner. The Navajo were kept on this barren land with few agricultural resources for four years before a new treaty eventually allowed them to go back to their land near Fort Defiance.

Barboncito, like many Indians, claimed that the reservation system had impoverished his once-wealthy people even though the Indians had cooperated fully with the government.

The bringing of us here has caused a great decrease of our numbers, many of us have died, also a great number of our animals. Our grand fathers had no idea of living in any other country except our own and I do not think it right for us to do so, as we were never taught to. When the Navajos were first created, four mountains and four rivers were pointed out to us, inside of which we should live. That was to be our country and was given to us by the first woman of the Navajo tribe. It was told to us by our forefathers, that we were never to move east of the Rio Grande or west of the San Juan rivers and I think that our coming here has been the cause of so much death among us and our animals.

That our God when we was created (the woman I spoke of) gave us this piece of land and created it specially for us and gave us the whitest of corn and the best of horses and

sheep. You can see them (*pointing to the other chiefs*) ordinarily looking as they are, I think that when the last of them is
gone the world will come to an end. It is true we were
brought here, also true we have been taken good care of
since we have been here. As soon as we were brought here
we started into work making acequias (and I myself went to
work with my party). We made all the Adobes you see here.
We have always done as we were told to. If told to bring
ashes from the hearth we would do so, carry water and herd
stock. We never refused to do anything we were told to do.
This ground we were brought on, it is not productive. We
plant but it does not yield. All the stock we brought here
have nearly all died.

This Ground Was Never Intended for Us

Because we were brought here, we have done all that we
could possibly do, but found it to be labor in vain, and have
therefore quit it. For that reason we have not planted or
tried to do anything this year. It is true we put seed in the
ground, but it would not grow two feet high, the reason I
cannot tell, only if I think that this ground was never intended for us. We know how to irrigate and farm, still we
cannot raise a crop here. We know how to plant all kinds of
seed, also how to raise stock and take care of it. The Commissioners can see themselves that we have hardly any sheep
or horses. Nearly all that we brought here have died, and
that has left us so poor that we have no means wherewith to
buy others.

There are a great many among us who were once well
off now they have nothing in their houses to sleep on except
gunny sacks. True, some of us have a little stock left yet, but
not near what we had some years ago in our old country.
For that reason my mouth is dry and my head hangs in sorrow to see those around me who were at one time well off,
so poor now. When we had a way of living of our own, we
lived happy. We had plenty of stock. Nothing to do but look
at our stock, and when we wanted meat, nothing to do but
kill it.

(Pointing to chiefs present)
They were once rich. I feel sorry at the way I am fixed
here. I cannot rest comfortable at night. I am ashamed to go
to the commissary for my food. It looks as if somebody was
waiting to give it to me. Since the time I was very small un-

til I was a man when I had my father and mother to take care of I had plenty and since that time I have always followed my fathers advice and still keep it. Viz: to live at peace with everybody. I want to tell the Commissioners I was born at the lower end of Canon-de-Chelle.

We have been living here five winters. The first year we planted corn it yielded a good crop, but a worm got in the corn and destroyed nearly all of it. The second year the same. The third year it grew about two feet high when a hail storm completely destroyed all of it. We have done all we possibly could to raise a crop of corn and pumpkins but we were disappointed. I thought at one time the whole world was the same as my own country but I got fooled in it. Outside my own country we cannot raise a crop, but in it we can raise a crop almost anywhere. Our families and stock there increase. Here they decrease.

This Land Does Not Like Us

We know this land does not like us neither does the water. They have all said this ground was not intended for us. For that reason none of us have attempted to put in seed this year. I think now it is true what my forefathers told me about crossing the line of my own country. It seems that whatever we do here causes death. Some work at the acequias, take sick, and die. Others die with the hoe in their hands. They go to the river to their waists and suddenly disappear. Others have been struck and torn to pieces by lightning. A Rattlesnake bite here kills us. In our own country a Rattlesnake before he bites, gives warning, which enables us to keep out of its way. And if bitten we readily find a cure. Here we can find no cure.

When one of our big men die, the cries of the women causes the tears to roll down onto my moustache. I then think of my own country. I think the Commissioners have seen one thing. When we came here there was plenty of mosquito root which we used for fuel. Now there is none nearer than the place where I met the Commissioners, 25 miles from here, and in winter many die from cold and sickness and overworking in carrying wood such a long distance on their backs. For that reason we cannot stay contented where we now are.

Some years ago I could raise my head and see flocks of cattle in any direction. Now I feel sorry I cannot see any. I raise my head and can see herds of stock on my right and left but they are not mine. It makes me feel sorry thinking of the time when I had plenty. I can scarcely endure it. I think that all nations round here are against us. (I mean Mexicans and Indians.) The reason is that we are a working tribe of Indians, and if we had the means we could support ourselves far better than either Mexican or Indian. The Comanches are against us. I know it for they came here and killed a good many of our men. In our own country we knew nothing about the Comanches. Last winter I heard said that there was a Commission coming here. Now I am happy it has arrived for I expect to hear from that Commission today the object of its coming here.

My mouth is dry and my head hangs in sorrow to see those around me who were at one time well off, so poor now.

We have all declared that we do not want to remain here any longer. If I can complete my thoughts today I will give the General my best thanks and think of him as my father and mother. As soon as I heard of your coming I made three pair of moccassins and have worn out two pair of them since. As you see yourselves, I am strong and hearty and before I am sick or older I want to go and see the place where I was born. Now I am just like a woman, sorry like a woman in trouble. I want to go and see my own country. If we are taken back to our own country we will call you our father and mother. If you should only tie a goat there we would all live off it, all of the same opinion. I am speaking for the whole tribe, for their animals from the horse to the dog, also the unborn. All that you have heard now is the truth and is the opinion of the whole tribe. It appears to me that the General commands the whole thing as a god. I hope therefore he will do all he can for the Indian. This hope goes in at my feet and out at my mouth I am speaking to you, General Sherman, now as if I was speaking to a spirit, and I wish you to tell me when you are going to take us to our own country.

Chapter 3

Breaking Up Indian Country (1884–1934)

1

The Reservation System Must Be Ended

Lyman Abbott

By the late nineteenth century, many Americans holding many different views were disgusted with the reservation system. Efforts to move the Indians onto reservations and keep them there had led to decades of bloody Indian Wars. These efforts were costing Americans a great deal of money. This angered many pragmatic citizens. Another faction wanted to see Indians become assimilated into American society and saw the reservations as hindrances. Isolated from the proper "civilizing" influences, reservation Indians were receiving neither the means to become Americanized nor to develop self-sufficiency. Still other people perceived the reservations as containing great amounts of wasted land—land that they thought could be better used by white settlers to establish homes and communities.

In the 1880s and 1890s people were calling for reform—or even abolition—of the reservation system. Many reformers had advocated establishing more civilizing influences and resources on the reservations. In fact, in 1872 Congress had turned over the role of Indian agent to Christian missionaries, thinking that would end the corruption rampant in the Indian agent system and would bring the civilizing Christian influence to the "uncivilized" race.

But some reformers thought this approach did not go far enough. Lyman Abbott, a well-known Congregational clergyman, writer, and reformer, was one of many who believed the country would be better off without the reservations. Abbott belonged to an influential organization called the Indian Rights Association. Ironically, no members were Indians and

Lyman Abbott, in proceedings of the Third Annual Meeting of the Lake Mohonk Conference, 1885.

the "rights" this organization promoted consisted of one: the right of the Indians to be completely assimilated into American society. (In fact, one IRA member, Richard Henry Pratt, founder of the Carlisle Indian Industrial School, made famous the motto "Kill the Indian, save the man.") The IRA felt that if Indians were properly educated and lived among white citizens instead of on isolated reservations, they would become Christianized and Americanized more quickly.

In the following speech, Lyman Abbott expresses his views that Americans have no obligation to keep their word in immoral treaties, that reservations are not improving the Indians' lot, and that reservations are holding back the advance of civilization and should be eliminated.

In 1887, Congress did abolish reservations. It passed the Dawes Act, also called the General Allotment Act. This law ended tribal government, allotted 160-acre plots of land to individual Indians, and allowed the government to sell all remaining reservation land.

In the first place, Mr. Chairman and ladies and gentlemen, there are one or two things we may take for granted:

We may take it for granted that we are not here to criticise legislation—certainly not those who have been laboring in the earlier periods of this movement against bitter hostility, sometimes open and avowed, and sometimes, hard to meet,—secret. We think it an honor that we are permitted to be enrolled with them, and we recognize gratefully the services they have rendered, are rendering, and have yet to render. In what I shall say this morning I hope I shall not be understood as criticising the Coke bill. So far as I understand it, it has my hearty and warm approval. I shall be glad to vote with the Conference an expression of that approval.

In the second place, it may be taken for granted that we are Christian men and women; that we believe in justice, good-will, and charity, and the brotherhood of the human race. At least none of us here desire to break the Ten Commandments, nor break down honor and rectitude. I think it may be taken for granted that all of us here are—I will not say friends of the Indian, but friends of humanity, and friends of equal rights; that there is no person invited here, and no one who has come, who desires for one moment, having sworn to his own hurt, to change, or alter, or break a contract or a treaty that he may be benefited by the breaking of it. But if we have made a bad contract it is better broken than kept. I do not propose to argue the question of treaty at any length, but it is proper to state the position I hold, with some others, on this subject.

We Must Do the Right Thing

It is not right to do a wrong thing, and if you have agreed to do a wrong thing, that agreement does not make it right. If we have made contracts the result of which, as shown by later experience, is inhumanity and degradation, we are not bound to go on with them—we are bound to stop. A few years ago the United States Government was giving scalping-knives to the Indians. No matter on what parchment the treaty was made, we were bound to stop the issue of the scalping-knives. If we had agreed with some tribe in ancient time that we would set up no school-house or church with them, we should have no right to go on with that treaty. If we have bound a millstone about the neck of the Indian, the first step of justice is to cut the cord and set him free. We have no right to keep a drunken Indian in darkness because we have agreed to do so till he has learned the evil effects of whiskey. The people of these United States made a sacred compact with one another— the Constitution of the United States—and we were told by the highest judicial and constitutional authorities that the Constitution required us to catch and return the fugitive slave. There were some who believed in a higher law—and I was one of them—under which no contract could be executed that made it our duty to become bloodhounds to pursue a fleeing man. We have no right to do a wrong because we have covenanted to. With these brief words on the subject of treaty making, I pass to the larger question, because our obligations to the Indian are not primarily rooted in contract or treaty. Our primary obligations to the Indian are of a much more fundamental character—the duties that the strong owe to the weak; that the Government owes to those under it; that man owes to his fellow man. We have no contract with the negro; but we owe duties to him. We have no contract with the Chinaman; but I think we owe him something. We have no contract with the Italian, the Hungarian, and others; yet we owe them duties. It is of these larger duties we owe that I speak this morning.

The Indians did not occupy this land. A people do not occupy a country simply because they roam over it.

When our fathers landed on these shores, there was no alternative but to make treaties with the Indians; it was necessary. We have now passed beyond the epoch in which it is right or necessary to make treaties, and have so officially declared. We can no longer be bound by our forefathers; we must adapt our policy to the change of circumstances. It is sometimes said that the Indians occupied this country and that we took it away from them; that the country belonged to them. This is not true. The Indians did not occupy this land. A people do not occupy a country simply because they roam over it. They did not occupy the coal mines, nor the gold mines, into which they never struck a pick; nor the rivers which flow to the sea, and on which the music of a mill was never heard. The Indians can scarcely be said to have occupied this country more than the bisons and the buffalo they hunted. Three hundred thousand people have no right to hold a continent and keep at bay a race able to people it and provide the happy homes of civilization. We do owe the Indians sacred rights and obligations, but one of those duties is not the right to let them hold forever the land they did not occupy, and which they were not making fruitful for themselves or others.

Reservation Boundaries Hold Back Civilization

The reservation system has grown up. It is not necessary to go into the process by which it has grown. It is enough to say that a territory in this country about twice as large as the entire territory of England, Ireland, and Scotland has been set apart to barbarism by the reservation system. The railroad goes to the edge of it and halts. The postoffice goes to the edge of it and halts. There are mines there unopened, great wealth untouched by those who dwell there. The reservation system runs a fence about a great territory and says to civilization, "Keep off!" It was a great complaint against William the Conqueror that he preserved great forests in the heart of his country for his hunting-ground. We have no right to preserve a territory twice as large as Great Britain for a hunting-ground for any one. If this reservation system was only doing a positive injury to us, then we might endure it. But it holds back civilization and isolates the Indian, and denies him any right which justice demands for him. What are you and I entitled to ask for, living under these stars and stripes? Protection for our homes; protection to go where we wish; a right to buy in the cheapest market; a right to education; the right to appeal to the protection of law; protection for ourselves and children. There is not one of these rights that the reservation system does not put its foot upon. Even under the modified system, modified by recent reforms, the United States says to the Indian, "You cannot have a home till half or two-thirds of your tribe will agree." Last night the *New York Times* said that the cowboys were watching along the borders of a distant reservation, waiting to shoot the first Indian that should appear; and unless rumor does the cowboy injustice, his bullet *might* fly across and hit an Indian before leaving his border. The Indian may not carry his goods across the reservation. We deny him an open market. Every right to which we hold ourselves entitled by the God of Heaven, we deny the Indian under this system, and expect to compensate him by putting in here a church and there a school-house. But Christianity is not merely a thing of churches and school-houses. The post-office is a Christianizing institution; the railroad, with all its corruptions, is a Christianizing power, and will do more to teach the people punctuality than schoolmaster or preacher can. I hope you will not think I speak in disrespect of church and school-house. They that are maintaining the church and school-house in those distant reservations are the very ones, without exception, that urge us to break down the barriers and let in the full flood-tide of Christian civilization. Theirs is the appeal, theirs the urgency. We take a few Indians and bring them to Carlisle and Hampton. Captain Pratt at Carlisle and General Armstrong at Hampton have done more for the Indian race—thank God for them!—than any man can do with a glib tongue or a quick pen. But General Armstrong has told us this year how this reservation system stands against his work, and Captain Pratt tells us the same. You educate an Indian boy and send him back to the Indian Territory. He must not find a wife here, because that would be "intermingling" with the American population. He looks for a wife there, and they look with as natural disgust upon a beaver hat as he would upon a squaw's blanket. These men, whether in the Territory or out of it, are rowing their boat against the whole tide of our national life and begging us to make it flow the other way.

The Reservation System Must Be Remade

I declare my conviction then that the reservation system is hopelessly wrong; that it cannot be amended or modified; that it can only be uprooted, root, trunk, branch and leaf, and a new system put in its place. We evangelical ministers believe in immediate repentance. I hold to immediate repentance as a national duty. Cease to do evil, cease instantly, abruptly, immediately. I hold that the reservation barriers should be cast down and the land given to the Indians in severalty; that every Indian should be protected in his right to his home, and in his right to free intercourse and free trade, whether the rest of the tribe wish him so protected or not that these are his individual, personal rights, which no tribe has the right to take from him, and no nation the right to sanction the robbery of. Do you ask, "What would you do to-morrow morning?" We are told that upon the Pacific coast is a tribe of Indians to which patents have been issued, and that these patents are in pigeon-holes in Washington. I would take them out to-morrow and send them to the Indians as fast as the railroad trains can carry them, and I would follow this work up all along the line. I would begin at once a process for the survey and allotment of land to individuals in severalty. I would take the Indian and give him the rights of manhood with this great American people; and if there are any tribes so wild and barbaric that this cannot be done with them, I would put them under close surveillance, and would bring them under a compulsory educative process.

I declare my conviction then that the reservation system is hopelessly wrong.

One word more. It is said that this is not safe; that we must protect the Indian. There are two methods for the protection of the Indian. They were proposed, some fifteen or twenty years ago, for the protection of the negro. A portion of the community believed the wisest thing to do was to place the negroes together in one State, separating them from the rest of the people and massing them on a great reservation, and if it did not cost too much, perhaps sending them to Liberia. This was to protect them from the wrongs their neighbors might do them. But the American people said "No! we will make these men free, we will give them the ballot, and they must protect themselves." We said to the negro just what Gen. Whittlesey said he would do with the Indian; and what St. Paul said eighteen centuries ago I would say still: "If a man will not work, neither shall he eat." In the case of the negro, though there were wrongs perpetrated, yet as the final result, the negro and the white man are adjusting their relations, and coming into harmony. I believe it safer to leave the Indian to the protection of the law than to the protection of the agency. For my part, I would rather run my risk with the laws of the land, and with the courts open to me, than with the agent, who may be a philanthropist or who may be a politician. We have made progress; we are making progress, but I am sometimes a little impatient, the progress is so slow. I feel a little as Horace Mann did when he came in after attending a convention, full of nervous impetuosity and wrathful at the slowness of the reform. Some one said to him, "God is patient." "Yes," he said, "God is patient, but I cannot wait."

2
Allotment Benefits the Indians

Luther Standing Bear

Just as the general American population disagreed about the place of reservations, so did Indians. When Congress passed the Dawes Act in 1887 (also called the General Allotment Act), Indians disagreed about what to do about it. Without any input from them, the government had decided to break up the reservations, allotting a certain amount of land to each Indian and selling the rest to settlers. In addition, the Dawes Act dissolved tribal government and made the Indians subject to the same laws as other Americans—although they would not be citizens nor would they have voting rights for at least twenty-five years. For the act to take effect, the tribes had to formally agree to it.

The rationales behind the Dawes Act were many. Those who considered themselves the Indians' friends saw the Dawes Act as fostering Indian assimilation into white society. Others simply wanted to obtain the land they felt the Indians were underutilizing.

On the Indians' part, while most had not wanted to move to reservations to begin with, some of them had now lived there for many years and did not want to be uprooted once again when they were assigned to their allotment. Additionally, if they signed the treaty they would be signing away a portion of their tribe's land—every acre that was not specifically allotted to tribe members could be sold or used by the government.

Another problem for the Indians was that reservation land was held by the tribe in common. Individual Indians might raise crops or graze livestock on a certain part, but they did not have individual ownership. The tribe decided together what was to

Excerpted from *My People, the Sioux* (Cambridge, MA: Houghton Mifflin, 1928) by Luther Standing Bear. Copyright © 1928 by Luther Standing Bear.

be done with the land. To many Indians, the idea of individual ownership was foreign and unsettling.

Some Indians saw allotment as advantageous. They believed allotment would give those who worked hard the opportunity to succeed in a way they could not while on the reservation.

The following article is taken from the memoirs of Luther Standing Bear, an Oglala Sioux. His father was a storekeeper on their reservation and was in favor of the allotment. In this selection, Luther Standing Bear recalls the events surrounding his band's reaction to the allotment vote. Luther Standing Bear belonged to a relatively prosperous and progressive family. He was one of the first to attend the Carlisle Indian Industrial School operated by Richard Henry Pratt, a career army man who believed that strictly focused education could enable Indians to assimilate successfully into white society.

The Government sent some commissioners out to our reservation. The object was to investigate allotments. All the chiefs were against the allotment proposition. They figured that they were to be given a piece of land, fenced in like a white man, but they were to have no openings to and from the land, and would starve.

The agent sent out word for all the Indians to come to the agency. Soon they came trooping in from all directions and made their camps, waiting for the council to open. Of course all the chiefs who imagined they knew something about this allotment proposition had spoken to the other Indians about it, and they all agreed that there was to be no more signing of any more papers for the white man.

But my father was in favor of the allotment. He had listened while I explained it to him. So he paid no attention to either the commissioners or the agent, but went alone to the council held by the Indians while they were waiting. Here several of the old chiefs arose to talk. My father also arose, and as he faced the others, they waited to hear first what he had to say. He spoke as follows:

Allotment Is Good

'My friends, there are some white men here from the Great Father at Washington. They have come to see us about an agreement concerning an allotment of land. Now, my son has explained the proposition to me, and I consider that it is a very good one. We are to receive a piece of land, three hundred and twenty acres, which will be surveyed. This is for farming. We are also to get a team of horses, a farm wagon, a milk cow, farming implements, and fifty dollars in cash toward building a house. This land we live on is not good for farming, because the seasons are not right for it. So I am going to ask the commissioners for a full section of land, six hundred and forty acres. If they will give us this, in addition to the other things mentioned, we should sign the paper. Our tribe is to receive three million dollars for this land, half of which is to be used to educate our children, and the balance is to be paid to us within twenty-five years. If we take a piece of land it will be ours forever. If any of you old men die, under present conditions, you have nothing you can leave your children. But if you have a piece of land, it will be theirs when you are gone. No one can take it from them. So I am in favor of accepting this land!'

Then Chief Hollow Horn Bear arose. He was against the allotment. He was the husband of my oldest sister Wastewin, the daughter of my mother by her first husband. He liked my father, but he was the head of his own band, and had a right to his opinion. He spoke as follows:

'My friends, you have all heard what my father-in-law says, but I do not think he is right. He believes what the white people tell him; but this is only another trick of the whites to take our land away from us, and they have played these tricks before. We do not want to trust the white people. They come to us with sweet talk, but they do not mean it. We will not sign any more papers for these white men!'

Many Opposed the Allotment

All the Indians grunted 'Hau!' ('How!'), which meant that they agreed with what Hollow Horn Bear said. Then other chiefs arose and spoke. So many of them were against the allotment that it seemed we were not to get it. But these councils which the Indians held among themselves were not recorded, as there were no white persons present.

Finally the Indians became so determined not to favor the allotment that they agreed that the first Indian who signed any more papers for the white men would be shot

Chiricahua Apache students pose for this photograph in 1886 after four months of training at the Carlisle Indian School in Pennsylvania.

down. While many of the Indians really agreed with my father, they were afraid to say so for fear of the consequences.

At last the day arrived for the meeting at the agency. All the chiefs and headmen, as well as all the Indians, were gathered together to listen to what the white men had to say. General George Crook, the famous army officer, was the first man to talk. He explained all about what the Indians were to receive, how the children were to be educated, etc. He mentioned the Carlisle School, and the good being accomplished there by Captain Pratt. He was followed by other white men, who asked the Indians if they did not think this was a good thing for them.

Then one of the Indians arose and said they did not fully understand things yet, but if the agent would furnish them with food, they would hold another council, and then they might consider what to do, to which the agent agreed. As soon as the Indians reached their tipis, they held another council.

The following day everybody was at the agency again. The commissioners again spoke, and were followed by several of the other Indians. Chief Hollow Horn Bear, who was against the allotment, spoke as follows:

'You white men have come to us again to offer something to us which we do not fully understand. You talk to us very sweet, but you do not mean it. You have not fulfilled any of the old treaties. Why do you now bring another one to us? Why don't you pay us the money you owe us first, and then bring us another treaty?'

Other chiefs followed and expressed their opinions of the treaties that had not been fulfilled. They argued that if they signed this treaty, then the old treaties would be forgotten. The commissioners tried to explain that the new treaty would be on the same footing with the others—that they were to receive their annuity goods just the same, as well as what was now being promised. However, the Indians did not believe this, so they said they would go home and think it over. They left, and then held another council between themselves alone. My father attended all these councils among the Indians, as well as those held with the commissioners. But he had already told the Indians what his own opinion was about the matter, and what his decision was, and he never spoke of it again; the Indians knew his decision was final.

There was one man in our tribe who never attended any of the councils. His name was Crow Dog—the Indian who shot and killed Chief Spotted Tail. He was permitted by the Government to carry a six-shooter at all times to protect himself. But at all gatherings of Indians—no matter if whites were present—he did not come. He was afraid to do so. However, he heard about my father's talk, and really believed he was right, although he did not dare to say so openly.

'For the Good of Your Children'

The day arrived for the third council with the Indians and commissioners. General Crook made a very strong speech. He told the Indians that they could consider him as their friend. 'Some of you have known me for a long time,' he stated, 'and you can trust me. When the President at Washington asked me to come to you with this proposition, I was glad to do so, because I know it is for your good and the good of your children. We know there are some men in the tribe who are in favor of this proposition, so to-morrow we will hold a meeting in order that you may have a chance to sign this paper. Those who do not believe it will not sign it.'

Everybody wondered just what he meant when he said

he knew some men in the tribe were in favor of this treaty. It was well known that my father favored it, but it was also known that he never hung around the commissioners. But news travels just the same.

The following day my father, with several of his friends, went to the agency. All the Indians gathered together as before, but this time they came carrying weapons. The commissioner again spoke, and then he asked if any one present had anything to say. My father thereupon arose and spoke about like this:

'My friends, you all know I have spoken to you about this treaty, because the way my son explained it to me it seemed good for our children and their children in turn. Some day they will have to mix with the white race; therefore, they will need an education. These men have told these things in the way my son told me, and I believe it. So I am going to sign this treaty.'

My Father Signs

Then shouts of 'Kill him! Kill him!' went up all over the hall; but my father never even turned his head. He walked straight to the table and touched the pen. That was his signature, as he had no education and could not write. My father's friends became very excited, and kept looking hither and thither. One man had his gun raised, ready to shoot, but some of the men picked him up bodily and threw him out of the hall. My father was the first man to sign the treaty in public, risking his life that we, his children, might receive an allotment of land from the Government.

'These men have told these things in the way my son told me, and I believe it. So I am going to sign this treaty.'

The other Indians saw that my father signed the paper without getting shot, so they began to have more courage. One after another started for the table and touched the pen. Soon the white men had to get other tables, as the Indians came so fast there was not room at one table. How happy my father was in knowing that the whole tribe believed he was doing the right thing for his people.

Several of the Indians who were not in favor of the treaty walked out of the council hall, among them being my brother-in-law, Chief Hollow Horn Bear. The commissioners remained a few days longer on the reservation, and other Indians, from time to time, came up to sign the treaty. As soon as most of the big men of the tribe had signed the paper, the commissioners went back to Washington. Nobody had been injured, but it took considerable courage to make the first move and be first in line.

3

Allotment Punishes the Indians

D.W.C. Duncan

The Dawes Act, or General Allotment Act, did not affect the Five Civilized Tribes (Cherokee, Chickasaw, Choctaw, Creek, and Seminole) because of prior treaty agreements that the government did not want to break. But in 1898 Congress passed the Curtis Act, which had the same effect. Historian Angie Debo reports that it "authorized the allotment of [the Five Tribes'] land, the division of their other property, and the termination of their governments." These laws also set major restrictions on what the Indians could do with their allotment.

A major purpose of the Dawes and Curtis Acts was to "divide and conquer"—they were designed to end "the Indian problem" by turning the communal tribes into disparate individuals. Some hoped the Indians would become seamlessly integrated into white American society by virtue of their new status as individual landowners, while others merely wanted to end the Indians' impediment to white expansion.

Despite the good intentions of many who supported the allotment acts, these laws did not benefit many Indians. As explained by D.W.C. Duncan, the speaker in the following testimony to the U.S. Senate, the impossible conditions imposed by the acts impoverished even those Indians who had been making progress under the old systems.

In order to make myself distinctly understood, gentlemen, it will be necessary to take you and carry you on a very brief glance over a page of Cherokee history, if you will give me the

D.W.C. Duncan, "Statement," Senate Report, no. 5013, 59th Cong., 2nd sess., Part 1, pp. 180–90, November 14, 1906.

time. A few decades ago, not more than forty years ago, the Cherokee Indian was the owner of a magnificent estate, including not less than 14,000,000 of the best acres that can be found now upon the American continent. The value of that land, upon a favorable market, was enough to give every man, woman, and child of the Cherokee people an ample competency for their life as long as they should live and a like provision to their posterity for a number of generations. But, to-day, what is the condition? All that I have, Senators, to-day, although I was part owner in that magnificent estate; all I own to-day is measured by the pitiful sum of $325. . . .

"Our Great Father at Washington, . . . smiled upon us . . . and we had hoped that those smiles would have been continued throughout the length of the period of time which was described to us a few years ago by President Jackson, "so long as grass grows and water flows," and we went to work and grass grew and water flowed and we lived in peace until Mr. Curtis, up here in Kansas, introduced a bill which was pushed through the forms of legislation at Washington, obliterating our tribal nation, abrogating our laws, extinguishing our treaties, rescinding our patents signed by the President of the United States, taking possession of our lands, placing the disposing power over it in the hands of the United States Government, which is nothing more nor less than fee-simple title. I might say that it practically transferred the title of our vast estate down here in the hands of the Government, and the Government assumed control over it and goes to disposing of it. In the first place, setting apart what is called reserves, thousands of acres for town sites, many acres for educational purposes, for churches and colleges, and I might go on and enumerate until every possible pretext for reserving the lands had been provided for and no more imaginable claims remaining to be gratified, and then, after the whole segregation was declared to be unallotable, we Indians, we Cherokees, we original owners of this land in fee simple under a solemn patent, come in as a last thing to be cared for, the very last thing; and then the Dawes Commission assigned us what? A piece of land valued at $325. . . .

Gentlemen, yesterday you heard some of those full bloods say like this—I think it was Joe Frog speaking to you through an interpreter; he threw out this idea; it is an idea which has been in my mind for years, ever since the Dawes Commission entered this Territory: "We can't afford to sell any of our land because we have not got enough. It is too small. If we sell any we will not have enough to maintain our families." As he was endeavoring to convey that fact another one of my fellow-countrymen, Mr. Glory, said: "Our people are in a bad fix." Those were his words, spoken in bad Indian language. Those words meant a great deal to people like us poor Indians. Our allotments are too small, and on the whole we are in a bad fix. Let me demonstrate my idea. . . .

Senators, just let me present to you a picture; I know this is a little digression, but let me present it. Suppose the Federal Government should send a survey company into the midst of some of your central counties of Kansas or Colorado or Connecticut and run off the surface of the earth into sections and quarter sections and quarter quarter sections and set apart to each one of the inhabitants of that county 60 acres, rescinding and annulling all title to every inch of the earth's surface which was not included in that 60 acres, would the State of Connecticut submit to it? Would Colorado submit to it? Would Kansas brook such an outrage? No! It would ruin, immeasurable ruin—devastation. There is not an American citizen in any one of those States would submit to it, if it cost him every drop of his heart's blood. That, my Senators, permit me—I am honest, candid, and fraternal in my feelings—but let me ask a question: Who is it that hastened on this terrible destruction upon these Cherokee people? Pardon me, it was the Federal Government. It is a fact; and, old as I am, I am not capable of indulging in euphuisms. . . .

What a condition! I have 60 acres of land left me; the balance is all gone. I am an old man, not able to follow the plow as I used to when a boy. What am I going to do with it? For the last few years, since I have had my allotment, I have gone out there on that farm day after day. I have used the ax, the hoe, the spade, the plow, hour for hour, until fatigue would throw me exhausted upon the ground. Next day I repeated the operation, and let me tell you, Senators, I have exerted all my ability, all industry, all my intelligence, if I have any, my will, my ambition, the love of my wife—all these agencies I have employed to make my living out of that 60 acres, and, God be my judge, I have not been able to do it. I am not able to do it. I can't do it. I have not been able to clear expenses. It will take every ear of the bounteous crop on that 60 acres—for this year is a pretty good crop year—it will take every bushel of it to satisfy the debts that

I have incurred to eke out a living during the meager years just passed. And I am here to-day, a poor man upon the verge of starvation—my muscular energy gone, hope gone. I have nothing to charge my calamity to but the unwise legislation of Congress in reference to my Cherokee people.

Incomparable Hardship

When I personate myself in this case—pardon me, Senators—I am speaking for the thousands of my fellow-citizens that are inhabiting those flint hills over there. This being the case, my own case, it doesn't begin to compare with the hardship with which those full bloods who spoke before you here yesterday have to contend. Compare—just take a practical view of the case—60 acres; suppose I put every acre of that 60 acres throughout into corn, and that is our staple production here, we have got to rely upon it—disregarding the space that I am to occupy for my dwelling, garden, hogpens, sheep pens, and things of that kind; suppose I put every acre of that tract into corn and raise a bountiful crop, twenty bushels to the acre. Let's see: That would be 1,200 bushels, which at 30 cents a bushel would be $360. I have been industrious, worked hard, been cheerful; I have whistled along on my way to the farm and back, told pleasant stories to my wife, and endeavored to be as chippery as I could. Now, I have my clothes to buy, the apparel of my wife and children, my grocery bill to settle, my taxes to pay, my repairs on my premises, if I have any—all to come out of that $360. You can figure that out yourself; I can't do it very well now in my mind. But I say this: There isn't a man in the State of Kansas that can get through the year with anything like reasonable comfort and respectability with $360 and pay all of his expenses. If he did get through with the skin of his teeth at the end of the year, he would merely be able to live and breathe, and nothing else. But will that condition satisfy a proud-spirited American citizen? Would one of you gentlemen be satisfied with that condition of things?

Put Yourself in Our Place

Suppose, gentlemen, an allotment scheme be put in force in your country and you be put in the same predicament; under this inexorable state of unchangeable affairs that you would never be able to have another acre but that, and if you can't live on it you can die on it. No! There isn't a citizen of the noble State of Kansas that would submit to it.

4

Americans Followed the Right Indian Policy

Theodore Roosevelt

Theodore Roosevelt was an adventurer, soldier, historian, and the twenty-sixth U.S. President (1901–1908). He was both an avid hunter and a conservationist, and, though he was an East-erner, he lived for a time on a North Dakota cattle ranch, writing about his experiences in such books as *Ranch Life and the Hunting-Trail*. In 1897, he organized and led the 1st U.S. Volunteer Cavalry, also called the Rough Riders, in the war with Spain over the Caribbean islands. Colorful and opinionated, he is remembered for his motto "Speak softly and carry a big stick."

In 1889, Roosevelt wrote the first edition of his best-selling history *The Winning of the West: An Account of the Exploration and Settlement of Our Country from the Alleghanies to the Pacific*. The book expressed Roosevelt's strong nationalism and showed how the Westward movement shaped the American character. Historian Gary Gerstle writes,

> Roosevelt's nationalism expressed itself as a combative and unapologetic racial ideology that thrived on aggression and the vanquishing of savage and barbaric peoples. . . . Yet, Roosevelt also located with American nationalism a powerful civic tradition that celebrated the United States as a place that welcomed all people, irrespective of their nationality, race, and religious practice, as long as they were willing to devote themselves to the nation and obey its laws.

In essence, Roosevelt believed the conflicts between Americans and Indians made America a stronger, more vital, and more unified nation. He admired Indian warriors—indeed, he admired all warriors—but his book makes clear that he had no regrets about the Indians' fate. He believed it was inevitable and right that Americans would expand throughout the North American continent and just as inevitable that the Indians would be exiled or exterminated if they did not become part of American society.

The Winning of the West was first published during a period when there was a great deal of controversy about U.S. treatment of the Indians. Among those who spoke out were several historians and political commentators who, Roosevelt felt, distorted history with their excessively liberal perspective. Roosevelt attached a brief appendix to his book decrying these historians and defending U.S. policy in spite of its admittedly sometimes harsh treatment of the Indians. The appendix, reprinted here, became a chapter note in later editions.

It is greatly to be wished that some competent person would write a full and true history of our national dealings with the Indians. Undoubtedly the latter have often suffered terrible injustice at our hands. A number of instances, such as the conduct of the Georgians to the Cherokees in the early part of the present century, or the whole treatment of Chief Joseph and his Nez Percés, might be mentioned, which are indelible blots on our fair fame; and yet, in describing our dealings with the red men as a whole, historians do us much less than justice.

It was wholly impossible to avoid conflicts with the weaker race, unless we were willing to see the American continent fall into the hands of some other strong power; and even had we adopted such a ludicrous policy, the Indians themselves would have made war upon us. It cannot be too often insisted that they did not own the land; or, at least, that their ownership was merely such as that claimed often by our own white hunters. If the Indians really owned Kentucky in 1775, then in 1776 it was the property of Boone and his associates; and to dispossess one party was as great a wrong as to dispossess the other. To recognize the Indian ownership of the limitless prairies and forests of this continent—that is, to consider the dozen squalid savages who hunted at long intervals over a territory of a thousand square miles as owning it outright—necessarily implies a similar recognition of the claims of every white hunter, squatter, horse thief, or wandering cattleman. Take as an example the country round the Little Missouri. When the cattlemen, the first actual settlers, came into this land in 1882, it was already scantily peopled by a few white hunters and trappers. The latter were extremely jealous of intrusion; they had held their own in spite of the Indians, and like the Indians, the inrush of settlers and the consequent destruction of the game meant their own undoing; also, again like the Indians, they felt that their having hunted over the soil gave them a vague prescriptive right to its sole occupation, and they did their best to keep actual settlers out. In some cases, to avoid difficulty, their nominal claims were bought up; generally, and rightly, they were disregarded. Yet they certainly had as good a right to the Little Missouri country as the Sioux have to most of the land on their present reservations. In fact, the mere statement of the case is sufficient to show the absurdity of asserting that the land really belonged to the Indians. The different tribes have always been utterly unable to define their own boundaries. Thus the Delawares and Wyandots, in 1785, though entirely separate nations, claimed and, in a certain sense, occupied almost exactly the same territory.

The Only Possible Policy

Moreover, it was wholly impossible for our policy to be always consistent. Nowadays we undoubtedly ought to break up the great Indian reservations, disregard the tribal governments, allot the land in severalty (with, however, only a limited power of alienation), and treat the Indians as we do other citizens, with certain exceptions, for their sakes as well as ours. But this policy, which it would be wise to follow now, would have been wholly impracticable a century since. Our central government was then too weak either effectively to control its own members or adequately to punish aggressions made upon them; and even if it had been strong, it would probably have proved impossible to keep entire order over such a vast, sparsely peopled frontier, with such turbulent elements on both sides. The Indians could not be treated as individuals at that time. There was no possible alternative, therefore, to treating their tribes as nations, exactly as the French and English had done before us. Our difficulties were partly inherited from these, our predecessors, were partly caused by our own misdeeds, but were mainly the inevitable result of the conditions under which the problem had to be solved; no human wisdom or virtue could have worked out a peaceable solution. As a nation, our Indian policy is to be blamed, because of the weakness it displayed, because of its short-sightedness, and its occasional leaning to the policy of the sentimental humanitarians; and we have often promised what was impossible to perform; but there has been little wilful wrong-doing. Our government almost always tried to act fairly by the tribes; the governmental agents (some of whom have been dishonest, and others foolish, but who, as a class, have been greatly traduced), in their reports, are far more apt to be unjust to the whites than to the reds; and the federal authorities, though unable to prevent much of the injustice, still did check and control the white borderers very much more effectually than the Indian sachems and war-chiefs controlled their young braves. The tribes were warlike and bloodthirsty, jealous of each other and of the whites; they claimed the land for their hunting-grounds, but their claims all conflicted with one another; their knowledge of their own boundaries was so indefinite that they were always willing, for inadequate compensation, to sell land to which they had merely the vaguest title; and yet, when once they had received the goods, were generally reluctant to make over even what they could; they coveted the goods and scalps of the whites, and the young warriors were always on the alert to commit outrages when they could do it with impunity. On the other hand, the evil-disposed whites regarded the Indians as fair game for robbery and violence of any kind; and the far larger number of well-disposed men, who would not willingly wrong any Indian, were themselves maddened by the memories of hideous injuries received. They bitterly resented the action of the government, which, in their eyes, failed to properly protect them and yet sought to keep them out of waste, uncultivated lands which they did not regard as being any more the property of the Indians than of their own hunters. With the best intentions, it was wholly impossible for any government to evolve order out of such a chaos without resort to the ultimate arbitrator—the sword.

Chapter **4**

Seesaw in the Twentieth Century (1934–1999)

1

Reform the Reservation System

Hamlin Garland

Within a decade or so of its passage, it was clear that the Dawes Act wasn't working in its aim of assimilating the Indians—though it had been very successful in reassigning "underutilized" reservation land to whites. (Judith Nies, author of *Native American History: A Chronology of a Culture's Vast Achievements and Their Links to World Events*, reports that "During the 40-year period of allotment [1887–1934], more than 86 million acres, over 60 percent of the remaining Indian landbase, passed into non-Indian hands.") Instead of becoming more Americanized and more self-reliant, many Indians were becoming more impoverished and more dependent on government help to survive. It seemed clear to many people that the Indians who, for the most part, had lived communally throughout their history, were not successfully adapting to the individualistic culture they were being forced to join.

Those who wished to help the Indians became more outspoken about the damage the Dawes Act and related allotment laws were causing. Where the allotment acts had done as much as possible to break up the tribal governments, destroy the Indians' cultural identity, and end the reservation system, now a movement to reestablish these things began. Novelist Hamlin Garland, author of the following article, was one of those who believed that to save the Indians and allow them to develop self-sufficiency, reservations would have to be revived. He felt this needed to be done by the Indians themselves as much as possible; if the government tried to impose standardized rules and tribal governments, the system would continue to fail. Garland was led to his conclu-

Hamlin Garland, "The Red Man's Present Needs," *North American Review*, April 1902.

sions by his travels around the country, during which he visited many reservations and saw how different the people of different tribes were. He concluded that a major part of the problem was that the government was trying to solve the "Indian problem" by treating all Indians alike. In actuality, Garland believed, the differences among the tribes and their reservations were so extreme as to make a blindly "equitable" system impossible. He proposed reforming the reservation system to account for tribal differences, provide instruction in farming and other necessary skills, encourage tribal arts, and treat Indians as citizens.

The views of Garland and others who wanted to see a return to tribal self-government finally prevailed. In the late 1920s Bureau of Indian Affairs director John Collier convinced millionaire John D. Rockefeller to finance a major study of conditions among the Indians. A team of social scientists under the leadership of John Meriam traveled from reservation to reservation for seven months. Their lengthy report pointed out the deplorable extent of the poverty, disease, and social maladjustment that permeated the Indian population, criticized the allotment acts as a major contributing factor, and recommended to Congress that the government end allotment and increase funding to support programs for Indian health and education. In 1934, Congress passed the Wheeler-Howard Act, also called the Indian Reorganization Act, which allowed tribes to reform their own governments, ended allotment, and encouraged the redevelopment of Indians' cultural identities through programs like the Indian Arts and Crafts Board, formed in 1934, which funded classes on reservations and helped market Indian products.

In the following excerpt Garland explains his views of tribal individuality. Garland was the author of harshly realistic novels and short stories, many of them with midwestern agricultural settings and didactic themes. Among the best known are *A Son of the Middle Border, A Daughter of the Middle Border,* and *Main-Travelled Roads.* He also wrote memoirs and *The Book of the American Indian,* a collection of Indian tales and legends.

I n my wanderings over the Rocky Mountain States, I have happened upon some twelve or fifteen Indian reservations. This unofficial inspection, made for fictional purposes, I now wish to turn to practical account in aid of a clearer understanding of the present conditions of the nation's wards. I am not to be taken as the representative of any organization whatsoever, and I have never held, and never sought, and do not intend to seek, any position under the government. Perhaps this freedom from departmental bias may lend a certain value to my statement of what I saw and what I think should be done. A part of what follows is necessarily critical, but its main intent is constructive. I do not doubt the good intention of the Indian Department; on the contrary, I believe its head to be sincerely anxious to clear the service of its abuses. What is here written is intended to aid rather than embarrass the Commissioner in getting rid of his inheritance of foolish policies.

It is necessary at the start to clear away the common misapprehension that "one Indian is precisely like another." This is not true. On the contrary, there are very wide divergencies of habit among the native tribes now living in America. Red men living side by side are as widely separated in speech and in manner as the Turk and the German. There are, indeed, two or three distinct races of Americans included under the term "Indian," speaking many languages quite distinct and irrelatable.

Reservations Are Open-Air Prisons

The second point to be grasped is this: There are no Indians living as nomads or hunters to-day. If the reader will examine a map of the United States Indian Department, he will find, scattered all over the West, minute, irregular patches of yellow, ranging from a thumb-nail's breadth to that of a silver quarter. These are the "corrals" or open-air prisons, into which the original owners of the continent have been impounded by the white race. Most of these reservations are in the arid parts of the great Rocky Mountain Plateau; a few are in timbered regions of older States, like Wisconsin and Minnesota. Speaking generally, we may say these lands are relatively the most worthless to be found in the State or Territory whose boundaries enclose the red man's home, and were set aside for his use because he would cumber the earth less there than elsewhere. Furthermore, scarcely a single one of these minute spots is safe to the red people. Every acre of land is being scrutinized, and plans for securing even these miserable plots are being matured.

All Tribes' Situations Are Not the Same

It will appear, even from a glance at this map, that to understand the "Indian problem," is to understand the climate, soil and surroundings of each one of fifty reservations, in a dozen States, hundreds, even thousands of miles apart, and to take into account the peculiarities of as many differing tribes of men. A rule which would apply perfectly to the Cheyennes of Oklahoma would not in the least apply to the Cheyennes of Montana, but might aid the Wichitas, Kiowas, or Fort Sill Apaches, not because the latter tribes are similar in habit, but because their soil, surroundings, and climate are practically the same.

The Sioux, Crows, Northern Cheyennes, Blackfeet, Gros Ventres, and Assiniboines, occupying respectively the Standing Rock reservation in Dakota, and the Crow, Tongue River, Fort Peck, Fort Belknap and Blackfeet reservations in Montana, are all in an arid climate and confronted with the problem of irrigation.

The Blackfeet, also a hunting race, have a land even less adapted to the raising of corn and wheat; for their reservation lies high on the eastern slope of the continental divide, and frosts blast both the growing and the ripening crop. They have, however, a good grass country and can be made self-supporting as herders. The Fort Peck reservation, in eastern Montana, on the upper Missouri, like the land at Standing Rock, Dakota, is upland prairie, with meagre streams and poor timber, a dry bleak land, fit only for stock-raising, except along the bottoms, where irrigation is possible.

The Crows are a little better off. They have abundant water from two beautiful streams, which take their rise in the Big Horn mountains; and they have put through some fairly successful irrigating ditches. They have also owned for several years herds of cattle; a cut in rations would not leave them helpless. The Northern Cheyennes, their neighbors, are in a rougher country, a very arid country, with only a few feeble streams, but they have plenty of timber and good grazing lands. Their chief needs are cattle, and a fence to keep out the cattle-men.

Misery for Some

The Sioux, the Blackfeet, and the Northern Cheyennes live practically the same life. They have small, badly-ventilated log or frame hovels of one or two rooms, into which they closely crowd during cold weather. In summer, they supplement these miserable shacks by canvas tepees and lodges, under which they do their cooking, and in which they sleep. Their home life has lost all its old-time picturesqueness, without acquiring even the comfort of the settler in a dugout. Consumption is very common among them, because of their unsanitary housing during cold weather.

They dress in a sad mixture of good old buckskin garments and shoddy clothing, sold by the traders or issued by the government. They are, of course, miserably poor, with very little to do but sit and smoke and wait for ration day. To till the ground is practically useless, and their herds are too small to furnish them support. They are not allowed to leave the reservation to hunt or to seek work, and so they live like reconcentrados. Their ration, which the government by an easy shift now calls a charity, feeds them for a week or ten days, and they go hungry till the next ration day comes round. From three to seven days are taken up with going after rations. These words also apply to the Jicarilla Apaches, and to a part of the Southern Utes. Chief Charley's followers have lands along Pine River which they irrigate. On some of these reservations lands are allotted, either actually or nominally, though the people make less account of it than the agent reports.

The red man is a sociable animal, and . . . his life, so far from being silent and sombre, has always been full of song and rich in social interchange.

The visitor among the Southern Cheyennes, Arapahoes, Kiowas, and Fort Sill Apaches, will find conditions quite other than those of the North. The climate is mild and the land very productive. Corn, cotton, fruit of all kinds, and wheat can be grown. The winters are short, and water and timber fairly abundant. With the exception of the Yakima and Flathead reservations, those in Oklahoma are the only really habitable Indian lands I have visited. Manifestly, a regulation which would do good in Oklahoma might work incalculable harm in Dakota and Montana. To cut rations among the Southern Cheyennes would prove only a temporary hardship; but a cut in rations among the Blackfeet or Sioux might result in actual starvation and death, or at least in slaughter of the small flocks of cattle which they have begun to cherish. There wide differences cannot be too often brought to departmental notice. . . .

Allotment Began in Land Lust

The allotment of lands in severalty which began in land-lust and is being carried to the bitter end by those who believe a Stone Age man can be developed into a citizen of the United States in a single generation, is in violent antagonism to every wish and innate desire of the red man, and has failed of expected results, even among the Southern Cheyennes, where the land is rich and climate mild because it presents a sombre phase of civilized life.

The attempt to make the Sioux a greedy land-owner, content to live the lonely life of the poor Western rancher, cut off from daily association with his fellows, is to me uselessly painful. If we would convert the primitive man to our ways, we must make our ways alluring.

We Can't Change Indians' Nature

We should not forget that the red man is a sociable animal, and that his life, so far from being silent and sombre, has always been full of song and rich in social interchange. All his duties—even his hunting—have always been performed in company with his fellows. He is a villager, never a solitary. He dreads solitude, and one of the old-time tribal punishments was to be thrust outside the camping circle. The life of every member of the tribe is open to comment. He confides every secret to his group of lodge-men. He shares his food, his tepee, with his fellows. It is this gregariousness of habit, this love of his kind, and this deep-seated dread of loneliness, which make the Sioux and the Cheyenne so reluctant to adopt the Dawes land theories. They cling to the lodge for the reason that it can be easily moved, and is cheap.

Naturally, those who were resolute to make the Indian a solitary took little thought of this deep-seated mental characteristic, being confident that resolute whacking would jar his brain-cells into conformity with those of a white man of the same age. With them the red hunter is not a man peculiar to his environment; he is merely a bad boy who obstinately goes wrong. That he loves running water, that he needs to be near wood for his fires, that he shrinks from the bleak, wind-swept prairies, are considerations of small account to them; but a man with many years experience among the Cheyennes said to me: "It is hard to make progress under the present system."

A Humane Plan

In the desire to make better Indians, and to make the transition from their old life to the new as easy as may be, to lessen rather than to add to the weight of their suffering, I offer the following suggestions:

First. Group the families of each tribe on the water courses of its reservation, in little settlements of four or five families, with their lands outlying, instead of forcibly scattering them over the bleak and barren uplands. The Standing Rock Sioux, Northern Cheyennes, and Assiniboines of Forts Peck and Belknap, could all be so colonized, and water drawn in from the streams upon their gardens,* while their cattle range in common. Why should not the Southern Cheyennes and Arapahoes, already on allotments along the streams, be allowed to draw together in villages if they please? The Northern Cheyennes, now in full possession of their streams, should retain these water rights in common. Individual occupancy of lots and individual ownership of products is all that is necessary to their colonization on the arable and irrigable land. Cattle of gentle breed should be given to them as the beginning of individual herds. The red man's feeling that the earth is for the use of all men, is right; he has always distinguished between the ownership of things and the ownership of land and water. It is possible to refine him without teaching him to be either greedy or stingy, just as we can emphasize the return to individual labor without forcing him to live as if in solitary confinement. I confess I have no sympathy with those who would make the red man suffer needlessly to fit their notion of discipline. As a boy, I hated the solitary labor of the Western farm, and I would not condemn even a convict to such life as is involved in a lonely cabin on the plains.

---

* The farmer at Poplar Creek two years ago showed me a garden of nearly one hundred acres which he had set aside in lots to some sixty or eighty men; and, though the season's water had been very meagre, he had been able to supply these families, through their own labor, with potatoes for the winter. He did more. He demonstrated that these people, with water for their lands, could be self-supporting in three years by means of a ditch costing not more than $50,000.

Change Reservation Structure

Second. Each reservation should be divided into districts, not too large, and a really competent man employed to personally teach the red men how to plow, sow, and reap. This essential part of the service is sadly inefficient. The "farmers" of the various agencies I have visited, are either ignorant or slothful, or they are so burdened with duties around the agency corrals, that they are hardly ever of marked use to the red men. The present working of the Civil Service has led to a vicious habit of "transferring" a bad or weak man from post to post. Furthermore, the employees in many cases are hold-overs, men who sought the service as a refuge and who remain in it because they are unfitted for other life. I am willing to admit, however, in justice to the department, that the pay is too small to secure the services of a really capable man, unless he assumes double duty, as among the Southern Cheyennes, where the farmers serve as sub-agents, or school superintendents, and have little time to give to field work. Part of the useless travel in this work of superintending would be removed by settlement in groups as above outlined, but an increase in the number of industrial teachers must be given before adequate instruction can be assured. The government would save money in the end.

The theory that to civilize the red man it is necessary to disrupt families . . . is so monstrous and so unchristian that its failure was foretold by every teacher who understood the law of heredity.

Life at most of the Indian agencies is not a joyous thing to contemplate. The buildings are bare, bleak barracks. The boarding-houses are vile, and amusements are few. It is not wonderful that refined natures shudder and flee at first glance. Only the chain of necessity keeps the average employee to his post. The Indian soon becomes a burden, a nuisance. Duties are mechanically performed, and each man permits his hand to fall short rather than to over-reach his exact duty. The effect of such service is not precisely inspiring to the Indian. The only ways to change this service are these—raise the standard of wages and make life pleasanter for those who isolate themselves to teach.

Provide a Wholesome Matron

Third. A vigorous, wholesome woman is needed in each district as matron. She ought not to be the wife of the farmer; her first duty should be the welfare of her wards, and she should have a genuine sympathy for them. As I go among the red people, the lack of a matron of this character seems the most crying omission of all. I have never seen this work properly done. It is, indeed, a sort of higher education. The women need to be taught by example how to cook and sew, how to keep house, how to bridge the chasm between the tepee fire and the cook-stove. The red people are like children in all these things; they cannot go beyond their teacher; they can only follow. If their "farmer" is ignorant and a loafer, and their matron slothful and ill-humored, they are involved in these vices. They are like children, also, in that each effort is quite sincere, though fitful. They are easily discouraged. They can reason, they do reason, and they want to do the right thing; but the mental habits fixed by thousands of years of a simpler life are hard to overcome. The man or woman called to teach them should be patient and a leader. It is not true to say that this work is being done in the schools. Working in "relays" in the laundry or kitchen of a boarding-house is quite different from taking care of a home after marriage. The field matron is needed to supplement the instruction in the schools.

Fourth. Wherever a tribe has a peculiar natural appetite for an art—as canoe-building, weaving, basket-making, or pottery-baking—the department should send among them a teacher capable of rescuing perishing forms and symbols, and able also to develop new forms built upon the old. The Jicarilla Apaches, for example, are fine basket-makers. This art, in place of being ignored or positively discouraged, as at present, should be at once seized as a means of benefiting the tribe. The growth of grass, willows or other material necessary for it should be cultivated and a market opened on just terms. *The value of such an art in maintaining the self-respect of a tribe cannot be over-estimated.* The Rev. W.C. Roe, a missionary at Seger's Colony, Oklahoma, is of the sort I can commend. He is employing this month seventy men and women making bead-work, tepees, bows and arrows, moccasins, and ornamental pouches—and what he has done can be duplicated by the agents and missionaries of other tribes. The

Navajo blankets and silver-ware, the Hopi and Tewan pottery, the Chippewa canoes, are all in demand, and the art of making them should be fostered. Life on most of the reservations is a grim contention against wind and sun and bare brown earth. Each condition should be minutely studied, and every favoring law seized upon. Whenever an industry can be developed along inherited aptitudes, it should be done.

Provide an Old Folks' Home

John Seger, who has been for many years a friend and teacher among the Arapahoes and Southern Cheyennes, pleads for an Old Folks' Home near his school, where the old people could spend the rest of their lives in peace near their grandchildren. They will not last long, but we cannot afford to let them suffer. Under Seger's plan a great part of their food would be raised in a garden, and they could be employed to teach their native arts to the young people. The licensed trader is a survival of the old rule and should be abolished. His monopoly is intolerable. Under the single restriction that no liquor should be sold, competing stores should be welcomed on each reservation, in order that the red man may sell his product to better advantage, as well as supply his needs at the lowest possible cost.

Fifth. Schools should be established in each "farm district," which should be at once boarding and industrial schools, like those at Colony and Red Moon, Oklahoma, and these schools should displace all sectarian and non-reservation schools whatsoever, and all forcible transportation of pupils to Eastern schools should instantly cease. The theory that to civilize the red man it is necessary to disrupt families and to smother natural emotions by teaching the child to abhor his parents, is so monstrous and so unchristian that its failure was foretold by every teacher who understood the law of heredity. The school should raise the parents with the child. Instruction should be most elementary, as it is at Seger, at Darlington, and at Red Moon, among the Southern Cheyennes. In these schools, the child is taught to grapple with the conditions of life on his own reservation. He is taught how to mend a harness and put it on a horse, not how to make a wagon; how to plant potatoes, not how to conjugate a Latin verb. After he has acquired the power to read and write and speak colloquially (which the Carlisle Indians I have met seldom do), he is taught the value of money, and sufficient arithmetic to enable him to transact the business of a herder or farmer. But admirable as this is, there are other possibilities. Wherever white and red are mingled as settlers, I would educate them in the little red school-house together, and this can soon be done in some parts of Oklahoma. In any case, the education should arm the child for his battle for life and should not alienate him from his people. "Honor thy father and thy mother," is a command which the red children implicitly obey, until they are taught that everything their poor old parents do is vile.

Reduce Missionary Indoctrinizing

Sixth. The missionaries in the field should be given to understand that they have no more rights in the premises than any other visitor, and that their attempt to regulate the amusements and the daily life of the red man is without sanction of federal authority. Many of the missionaries I have met are devoted souls, but I would not care to live where they had power to define what recreations were proper and what were not. Their view of "profane" songs and pleasures is absurdly narrow and (to put it mildly) inelastic. They do not represent the culture and scholarship of our day; and while I appreciate their motives and their sacrifices, I cannot but observe that they are often an embarrassment to the agent and sad examples of narrow piety. In the interest of their own influence, I would urge all Eastern Missionary Societies to at once impress upon their representatives on the reservations the wisdom of assisting in the preservation and development of the native arts of the tribe with which they are associated. This they can do with very little money, by inducing all the old men and women (who are the fast fading representatives of these arts) to instruct their sons and daughters, nieces or grandchildren, in silver-smithing, basket-making, blanket-weaving, or whatever form of work they know best. The parent society could also form itself into an agency for the sale of wares, being careful to keep the advice of accredited authorities on art in order that the product may not lose vogue by becoming cheap and characterless. Mr. and Mrs. Roe, of Seger's Colony, Oklahoma, are examples of missionaries with larger aims than merely making converts. Mr. Roe's influence is not due to his preaching of dogma, but to his kindliness and helpfulness as a man and brother.

As the number of settlers moving west increased, Native Americans were forced onto reservations.

This industrial side of the Indian problem fits in just now with the revival of handicraft so strikingly general throughout the nation, and it may be that in it lies a very considerable means of aiding the red man, as he painfully crosses the gulf between his old warrior life and his life as a cattle-herder and gardener. He cannot be cut off from all his past; progress is not of that nature; it proceeds by slow displacement, by gradual accretion. Above all, the red man must feel that he is worth while, that he is a man among men—different, but not despicable because different. We should try to make him an admirable red man, as Booker Washington is trying to make the negro an admirable black man.

Give Indians Citizens' Rights

Seventh. Wherever a red man takes his allotment, he should be considered a citizen, free to come and go as he pleases, subject to the same general laws as his white neighbor. He should be allowed to visit other reservations and inter-marry with other tribes; he will never inter-marry to any extent with the whites; he ought not to do so if he could. Under this new condition, the agent will no longer be the commander, but the friend, the adviser, the attorney; his authority will depend on his judgment, his tact, his helpfulness.

The present condition of the allottee is an anomalous one; he is neither man, brute, nor neighbor. He is told by the Commissioner that he is free to do as other men; but when he seeks to leave the reservation he is ordered back by the agent. He is forbidden to visit in numbers exceeding five or ten; he is ordered not to dance, admonished to wear his hair short. He is told that he must not use paint on his face, and a hundred other useless indignities and restrictions are put upon him;* and, if he protests, he is told that so long as he eats the rations of the government he must obey the agent; and yet these rations are not only his necessity, they are his due. I have sometimes felt that the red man is the most patient and long-suffering creature in the world. Those who cry out against "pauperizing" him by means of rations have little comprehension of the barren lands he inhabits, and the necessity and the justice of his allowance.

The present condition of the allottee is an anomalous one; he is neither man, brute, nor neighbor.

The allottee should be made a citizen in truth, subject to punishment when he goes wrong, free to dress as he

* The general effect of the legislation suggested by those who would convert the man of the Stone Age into a "Christian citizen" is something like this:

> "You, Whiteshield, will at once leave your pleasant camp in the grove beside the Washita and take yourself to your homequarter. You will at once give up the tepee and all your skin clothing. You will put off your moccasins and take to brogans. You will build a hut and live therein. You will have your hair cut short, and give up painting your face. You will cease all singing and dancing. Every form and symbol of the past is vile—put them away. You will send your children to school—even the little ones of five must go. Smoking is expensive, and leads to dreaming—stop it. To do bead-work or basket-weaving is heathen; your wife must abandon that. You will instantly begin to raise pigs and chickens, and work hard every day, because it is good to work. In order that you may know how sweet it is to live the life of the white farmer, you may go to church on Sunday and hear a man talk in words which you do not understand, and sing songs which white people sing when they have nothing better to do." This reads like a caricature, but I assure the reader it is only a condensation of the suggestions made in my hearing by kindly people who believed themselves to be Christians.

pleases and live as he pleases, so far as forceful change is concerned. He should be encouraged to live better, to dress in keeping with his fortunes. Religious bias should no longer control him. His rights as a man should be respected. I have no sympathy with those who would "break" the head man and discredit every native amusement, turning the tribe into a settlement of joyless hypocrites. The zealots who preach this are themselves losing power in the world. What sort of village would that be where sombre fanatics could regulate the amusements and the education of the citizens? A people must have play; and, until the young red men and women come naturally to enjoy baseball and the Virginia reel, the government is in cruel business when attempting to force relinquishment of native songs, games and dances.

Finally. The question of abolition of reservations comes up, and is advocated by those who would teach the red man to farm, as you teach a puppy to swim by flinging it into the river. "Let them sink, or paddle and keep afloat," they say, but to let down the bars on some of the reservations would be to submerge the tribe utterly and render it homeless. The reservation is still an "isle of safety" to the Northwest tribes.

2

It Is Time to Return Indian Rule to the Indians

Richard M. Nixon

By the 1950s, the pendulum of opinion on the Indian question had swung once again. The 1934 Indian Reorganization Act had recognized the importance of the tribe in the American Indian cultures and had reestablished reservation tribal governments. It had also established programs to support Indian education, health, and cultural preservation. But in the post–World War II era, all that changed. Historian Angie Debo attributes the change, at least in part, to "the envious eyes . . . again fixed on the Indians' land." The government and the Bureau of Indian Affairs (BIA) began to withdraw support from Indian programs, and the government began to speak of dissolving the "special relationship" between the government and the reservations. The idea, once again, was to end tribal government and make Indians individual citizens subject to the same state laws, privileges, and responsibilities as other citizens. Tribal governments would be terminated. There would no longer be tribal police and court systems. Reservation land would no longer be sacrosanct. Federal services and jurisdiction would be withdrawn.

The BIA began to draw up a list of those tribes ready to be "terminated"—generally the more economically successful tribes and those with land or natural assets that were attractive to the greater population. These included the Wisconsin Menominee and the Oregon Klamuth, whose combined reservations contained almost a million acres of valuable timber. But it also included four impoverished Utah Paiute bands who lived on 46,000 desert acres thought to be potentially oil- and uranium-rich.

Richard M. Nixon, "Special Message on Indian Affairs," *Public Papers of the Presidents of the United States: Richard Nixon, 1970* (Washington, DC: U.S. Printing Office, 1970).

Access to valuable land was not the only goal of termination. Political science professor Gary Orfield writes, "The idea was to 'liberate' Indians from reservations and the Bureau of Indian Affairs and to force them to become participants in what the advocates saw as the superior social and economic arrangements off the reservations."

By the 1960s, a time of extraordinary social activism in America, American Indians began to demonstrate against government treatment of Indians.

Organizations like the National Indian Youth Council (NIYC) and the militant American Indian Movement demanded the attention of the government and the public. As anthropologist Peter Nabakov writes, these groups

> were responding to grim realities of Indian life: an average death age of forty due to disease, alcoholism, and malnutrition; an infant mortality rate more than twice the national average; the highest teen and pre-teen suicide rate in America; liver disease from alcoholism five times higher than the white population, and Indians under twenty-four years of age dying from alcoholism at a rate twenty-eight times the national average; more than fifty thousand Indian families living in unsanitary shanties or abandoned cars.

In addition, Nabakov writes, the activists pointed to specific areas of contention, among which were the following:

> (1) In Upper New York State the Senecas were furious over the flooding of their valleys by the Kinzua Dam Project, a violation of one of the oldest U.S. treaties with Indians; (2) in Alaska both Eskimos and Indians were agitated over challenges to water rights; (3) in Washington State game wardens were stepping up arrests of Indian fishermen in a confrontation over fish and game laws; (4) in South Dakota Sioux groups were resisting the state's curtailment of the power of Indian reservation police; (5) in California the use of peyote cactus in rituals of the Native American Church came under new legal assault.

In the meantime, the government was slowly coming back around to the view that Indians would do best when allowed to keep their reservations and have a say in their own governments. Members of the tribes that had been terminated, many of them once wealthy, were now largely impoverished and landless. Statistics like those stated above demonstrated the inadequacy of federal programs designed to help the Indians adapt to white culture or to survive on the land that remained to them. They also reflect the inability of many Indians to adapt to a tribeless, capitalistic culture. Beginning in the early 1960s, various laws were passed that gradually provided more opportunity for self-determination. In 1964, for example, the Office of Economic Opportunity was authorized to bypass the always controversial Bureau of Indian Affairs and give funds directly to qualifying tribes to combat poverty. President Lyndon Johnson's Great Society programs included Indian tribes in their scope. Johnson also proposed to Congress that Indians should have "an opportunity to remain in their homelands, if they choose, without surrendering their dignity; an opportunity to move to the towns and cities of America, if they choose, equipped with the skills to live in equality and dignity."

Richard M. Nixon, the thirty-seventh president (1969–1974), carried on this policy of assisted self-determination. In 1970, he presented a detailed plan to Congress rejecting termination, providing for programs to help Indians attain self-sufficiency, supporting reservation economic development, and returning the sacred Blue Lake area to the Taos Pueblo. (The returned area included 48,000 acres in Carson National Forest, which held Blue Lake, a site sacred to the tribe. It had been taken from the Indians in 1906.) The following article is excerpted from a speech Nixon gave to Congress outlining these proposals.

To the Congress of the United States:

The first Americans—the Indians—are the most deprived and most isolated minority group in our nation. On virtually every scale of measurement—employment, income, education, health—the condition of the Indian people ranks at the bottom.

This condition is the heritage of centuries of injustice. From the time of their first contact with European settlers, the American Indians have been oppressed and brutalized, deprived of their ancestral lands and denied the opportunity to control their own destiny. Even the Federal programs which are intended to meet their needs have frequently proven to be ineffective and demeaning.

But the story of the Indian in America is something more than the record of the white man's frequent aggres-

sion, broken agreements, intermittent remorse and prolonged failure. It is a record also of endurance, of survival,
of adaptation and creativity in the face of overwhelming ob-
stacles. It is a record of enormous contributions to this
country—to its art and culture, to its strength and spirit, to
its sense of history and its sense of purpose.

It is long past time that the Indian policies of the Federal government began to recognize and build upon the ca-
pacities and insights of the Indian people. Both as a matter
of justice and as a matter of enlightened social policy, we
must begin to act on the basis of what the Indians themselves have long been telling us. The time has come to break
decisively with the past and to create the conditions for a
new era in which the Indian future is determined by Indian
acts and Indian decisions.

Self-Determination Without Termination

The first and most basic question that must be answered
with respect to Indian policy concerns the historic and legal
relationship between the Federal government and Indian
communities. In the past, this relationship has oscillated between two equally harsh and unacceptable extremes.

On the one hand, it has—at various times during previous Administrations—been the stated policy objective of
both the Executive and Legislative branches of the Federal
government eventually to terminate the trusteeship relationship between the Federal government and the Indian
people. As recently as August of 1953, in House Concurrent
Resolution 108, the Congress declared that termination was
the long-range goal of its Indian policies. This would mean
that Indian tribes would eventually lose any special standing
they had under Federal law: the tax exempt status of their
lands would be discontinued; Federal responsibility for their
economic and social well-being would be repudiated; and
the tribes themselves would be effectively dismantled.
Tribal property would be divided among individual members who would then be assimilated into the society at large.

This policy of forced termination is wrong, in my judgment, for a number of reasons. First, the premises on which
it rests are wrong. Termination implies that the Federal
government has taken on a trusteeship responsibility for Indian communities as an act of generosity toward a disadvantaged people and that it can therefore discontinue this

responsibility on a unilateral basis whenever it sees fit. But the unique status of Indian tribes does not rest on any premise such as this. The special relationship between Indians and the Federal government is the result instead of solemn obligations which have been entered into by the United States Government. Down through the years, through written treaties and through formal and informal agreements, our government has made specific commitments to the Indian people. For their part, the Indians have often surrendered claims to vast tracts of land and have accepted life on government reservations. In exchange, the government has agreed to provide community services such as health education and public safety, services which would presumably allow Indian communities to enjoy a standard of living comparable to that of other Americans.

This goal, of course, has never been achieved. But the special relationship between the Indian tribes and the Federal government which arises from these agreements continues to carry immense moral and legal force. To terminate this relationship would be no more appropriate than to terminate the citizenship rights of any other American.

Termination Policy Has Harmed the Indians

The second reason for rejecting forced termination is that the practical results have been clearly harmful in the few instances in which termination actually has been tried. The removal of Federal trusteeship responsibility has produced considerable disorientation among the affected Indians and has left them unable to relate to a myriad of Federal, State and local assistance efforts. Their economic and social condition has often been worse after termination than it was before.

The third argument I would make against forced termination concerns the effect it has had upon the overwhelming majority of tribes which still enjoy a special relationship with the Federal government. The very threat that this relationship may someday be ended has created a great deal of apprehension among Indian groups and this apprehension, in turn, has had a blighting effect on tribal progress. Any step that might result in greater social, economic or political autonomy is regarded with suspicion by many Indians who fear that it will only bring them closer to the day when the Federal government will disavow its responsibility and cut them adrift.

In short, the fear of one extreme policy, forced termination, has often worked to produce the opposite extreme: excessive dependence on the Federal government. In many cases this dependence is so great that the Indian community is almost entirely run by outsiders who are responsible and responsive to Federal officials in Washington, D.C., rather than to the communities they are supposed to be serving. This is the second of the two harsh approaches which have long plagued our Indian policies. Of the Department of the Interior's programs directly serving Indians, for example, only 1.5 percent are presently under Indian control. Only 2.4 percent of HEW's [Department of Health, Education, and Welfare] Indian health programs are run by Indians. The result is a burgeoning Federal bureaucracy, programs which are far less effective than they ought to be, and an erosion of Indian initiative and morale.

Of the Department of the Interior's programs directly serving Indians . . . the result is a burgeoning Federal bureaucracy [and] programs which are far less effective than they ought to be.

I believe that both of these policy extremes are wrong. Federal termination errs in one direction, Federal paternalism errs in the other. Only by clearly rejecting both of these extremes can we achieve a policy which truly serves the best interests of the Indian people. Self-determination among the Indian people can and must be encouraged without the threat of eventual termination. In my view, in fact, that is the only way that self-determination can effectively be fostered.

Recommendations

This, then, must be the goal of any new national policy toward the Indian people: to strengthen the Indian's sense of autonomy without threatening his sense of community. We must assure the Indian that he can assume control of his own life without being separated involuntarily from the tribal group. And we must make it clear that Indians can become independent of Federal control without being cut off from Federal concern and Federal support. My specific recommendations to the Congress are designed to carry out this policy.

1. *Rejecting Termination*

Because termination is morally and legally unacceptable, because it produces bad practical results, and because the mere threat of termination tends to discourage greater self-sufficiency among Indian groups, I am asking the Congress to pass a new Concurrent Resolution which would expressly renounce, repudiate and repeal the termination policy as expressed in House Concurrent Resolution 108 of the 83rd Congress. This resolution would explicitly affirm the integrity and right to continued existence of all Indian tribes and Alaska native governments, recognizing that cultural pluralism is a source of national strength. It would assure these groups that the United States Government would continue to carry out its treaty and trusteeship obligations to them as long as the groups themselves believed that such a policy was necessary or desirable. It would guarantee that whenever Indian groups decided to assume control or responsibility for government service programs, they could do so and still receive adequate Federal financial support. In short, such a resolution would reaffirm for the Legislative branch—as I hereby affirm for the Executive branch—that the historic relationship between the Federal government and the Indian communities cannot be abridged without the consent of the Indians.

2. *The Right to Control and Operate Federal Programs*

Even as we reject the goal of forced termination, so must we reject the suffocating pattern of paternalism. But how can we best do this? In the past, we have often assumed that because the government is obliged to provide certain services for Indians, it therefore must administer those same services. And to get rid of Federal administration, by the same token, often meant getting rid of the whole Federal program. But there is no necessary reason for this assumption. Federal support programs for non-Indian communities—hospitals and schools are two ready examples—are ordinarily administered by local authorities. There is no reason why Indian communities should be deprived of the privilege of self-determination merely because they receive monetary support from the Federal government. Nor should they lose Federal money because they reject Federal control.

For years we have talked about encouraging Indians to exercise greater self-determination, but our progress has never been commensurate with our promises. Part of the reason for this situation has been the threat of termination. But another reason is the fact that when a decision is made as to whether a Federal program will be turned over to Indian administration, it is the Federal authorities and not the Indian people who finally make that decision.

This situation should be reversed. In my judgment, it should be up to the Indian tribe to determine whether it is willing and able to assume administrative responsibility for a service program which is presently administered by a Federal agency. To this end, I am proposing legislation which would empower a tribe or a group of tribes or any other Indian community to take over the control or operation of Federally-funded and administered programs in the Department of the Interior and the Department of Health, Education and Welfare whenever the tribal council or comparable community governing group voted to do so.

Under this legislation, it would not be necessary for the Federal agency administering the program to approve the transfer of responsibility. It is my hope and expectation that most such transfers of power would still take place consensually as a result of negotiations between the local community and the Federal government. But in those cases in which an impasse arises between the two parties, the final determination should rest with the Indian community.

Indian Control of Indian Programs

Under the proposed legislation, Indian control of Indian programs would always be a wholly voluntary matter. It would be possible for an Indian group to select that program or that specified portion of a program that it wants to run without assuming responsibility for other components. The "right of retrocession" would also be guaranteed; this means that if the local community elected to administer a program and then later decided to give it back to the Federal government, it would always be able to do so.

Appropriate technical assistance to help local organizations successfully operate these programs would be provided by the Federal government. No tribe would risk economic disadvantage from managing its own programs; under the proposed legislation, locally-administered programs would be funded on equal terms with similar services still administered by Federal authorities. The legislation I propose would include appropriate protections against any action which endangered the rights, the health, the safety or the welfare of individuals. It would also contain account-ability procedures to guard against gross negligence or mis-management of Federal funds.

This legislation would apply only to services which go directly from the Federal government to the Indian com-munity; those services which are channeled through State or local governments could still be turned over to Indian control by mutual consent. To run the activities for which they have assumed control, the Indian groups could employ local people or outside experts. If they chose to hire Federal employees who had formerly administered these projects, those employees would still enjoy the privileges of Federal employee benefit programs—under special legislation which will also be submitted to the Congress.

I hereby affirm . . . that the historic relationship between the Federal Government and the Indian communities cannot be abridged without the consent of the Indians.

Legislation which guarantees the right of Indians to contract for the control or operation of Federal programs would directly channel more money into Indian communi-ties, since Indians themselves would be administering pro-grams and drawing salaries which now often go to non-Indian administrators. The potential for Indian control is significant, for we are talking about programs which annu-ally spend over $400 million in Federal funds. A policy which encourages Indian administration of these programs will help build greater pride and resourcefulness within the Indian community. At the same time, programs which are managed and operated by Indians are likely to be more ef-fective in meeting Indian needs.

I speak with added confidence about these anticipated results because of the favorable experience of programs which have already been turned over to Indian control. Un-der the auspices of the Office of Economic Opportunity

(OEO), Indian communities now run more than 60 community action agencies which are located on Federal reservations. OEO is planning to spend some $57 million in Fiscal Year 1971 through Indian-controlled grantees. For over four years, many OEO-funded programs have operated under the control of local Indian organizations and the results have been most heartening.

Two Indian tribes—the Salt River Tribe and the Zuni Tribe—have recently extended this principle of local control to virtually all of the programs which the Bureau of Indian Affairs has traditionally administered for them. Many Federal officials, including the Agency Superintendent, have been replaced by elected tribal officers or tribal employees. The time has now come to build on these experiences and to extend local Indian control—at a rate and to the degree that the Indians themselves establish.

3. *Restoring the Sacred Lands Near Blue Lake*

No government policy toward Indians can be fully effective unless there is a relationship of trust and confidence between the Federal government and the Indian people. Such a relationship cannot be completed overnight; it is inevitably the product of a long series of words and actions. But we can contribute significantly to such a relationship by responding to just grievances which are especially important to the Indian people.

One such grievance concerns the sacred Indian lands at and near Blue Lake in New Mexico. From the fourteenth century, the Taos Pueblo Indians used these areas for religious and tribal purposes. In 1906, however, the United States Government appropriated these lands for the creation of a national forest. According to a recent determination of the Indian Claim Commission, the government "took said lands from petitioner without compensation."

For 64 years, the Taos Pueblo has been trying to regain possession of this sacred lake and watershed area in order to preserve it in its natural condition and limit its non-Indian use. The Taos Indians consider such action essential to the protection and expression of their religious faith.

The restoration of the Blue Lake lands to the Taos Pueblo Indians is an issue of unique and critical importance to Indians throughout the country. I therefore take this opportunity wholeheartedly to endorse legislation which would restore 48,000 acres of sacred land to the Taos Pueblo people, with the statutory promise that they would be able to use these lands for traditional purposes and that except for such uses the lands would remain forever wild.

With the addition of some perfecting amendments, legislation now pending in the Congress would properly achieve this goal. That legislation (H.R. 471) should promptly be amended and enacted. Such action would stand as an important symbol of this government's responsiveness to the just grievances of the American Indians.

4. *Indian Education*

One of the saddest aspects of Indian life in the United States is the low quality of Indian education. Drop-out rates for Indians are twice the national average and the average educational level for all Indians under Federal supervision is less than six school years. Again, at least a part of the problem stems from the fact that the Federal government is trying to do for Indians what many Indians could do better for themselves.

The Federal government now has responsibility for some 221,000 Indian children of school age. While over 50,000 of these children attend schools which are operated directly by the Bureau of Indian Affairs, only 750 Indian children are enrolled in schools where the responsibility for education has been contracted by the BIA to Indian school boards. Fortunately, this condition is beginning to change. The Ramah Navajo Community of New Mexico and the Rough Rock and Black Water Schools in Arizona are notable examples of schools which have recently been brought under local Indian control. Several other communities are now negotiating for similar arrangements.

Consistent with our policy that the Indian community should have the right to take over the control and operation of federally funded programs, we believe every Indian community wishing to do so should be able to control its own Indian schools. This control would be exercised by school boards selected by Indians and functioning much like other school boards throughout the nation. To assure that this goal is achieved, I am asking the Vice President, acting in his role as Chairman of the National Council on Indian Opportunity, to establish a Special Education Subcommittee of that Council. The members of that Subcommittee should be Indian educators who are selected by the Council's Indian members. The Subcommittee will provide technical assistance to Indian communities wishing to establish school boards, will conduct a nationwide review of the educational status of all Indian school children in whatever schools they may be attending, and will evaluate and report annually on the status of Indian education, including the extent of local control. This Subcommittee will act as a transitional mechanism; its objective should not be self-perpetuation but the actual transfer of Indian education to Indian communities.

Helping Indian Children in Public Schools

We must also take specific action to benefit Indian children in public schools. Some 141,000 Indian children presently attend general public schools near their homes. Fifty-two thousand of these are absorbed by local school districts without special Federal aid. But 89,000 Indian children attend public schools in such high concentrations that the State or local school districts involved are eligible for special Federal assistance under the Johnson-O'Malley Act. In Fiscal Year 1971, the Johnson-O'Malley program will be funded at a level of some $20 million.

Programs which are managed and operated by Indians are likely to be more effective in meeting Indian needs.

This Johnson-O'Malley money is designed to help Indian students, but since funds go directly to the school districts, the Indians have little if any influence over the way in which the money is spent. I therefore propose that the Congress amend the Johnson-O'Malley Act so as to authorize the Secretary of the Interior to channel funds under this act directly to Indian tribes and communities. Such a provision would give Indians the ability to help shape the schools which their children attend and, in some instances, to set up new school systems of their own. At the same time, I am directing the Secretary of the Interior to make every effort to ensure that Johnson-O'Malley funds which are presently directed to public school districts are actually spent to improve the education of Indian children in these districts.

5. *Economic Development Legislation*

Economic deprivation is among the most serious of Indian problems. Unemployment among Indians is ten times the national average; the unemployment rate runs as high as 80 percent on some of the poorest reservations. Eighty percent of reservation Indians have an income which falls below the poverty line; the average annual income for such families is only $1,500. As I said in September of 1968, it is critically important that the Federal government support and encourage efforts which help Indians develop their own economic infrastructure. To that end, I am proposing the "Indian Financing Act of 1970."

This act would do two things:

1. It would broaden the existing Revolving Loan Fund, which loans money for Indian economic development projects. I am asking that the authorization for this fund be increased from approximately $25 million to $75 million.

2. It would provide additional incentives in the form of loan guarantees, loan insurance and interest subsidies to encourage *private* lenders to loan more money for Indian economic projects. An aggregate amount of $200 million would be authorized for loan guarantee and loan insurance purposes.

I also urge that legislation be enacted which would permit any tribe which chooses to do so to enter into leases of its land for up to 99 years. Indian people now own over 50 million acres of land that are held in trust by the Federal government. In order to compete in attracting investment capital for commercial, industrial and recreational development of these lands, it is essential that the tribes be able to offer long-term leases. Long-term leasing is preferable to selling such property since it enables tribes to preserve the trust ownership of their reservation homelands. But existing law limits the length of time for which many tribes can enter into such leases. Moreover, when long-term leasing is allowed, it has been granted by Congress on a case-by-case basis, a policy which again reflects a deep-rooted pattern of paternalism. The twenty reservations which have already been given authority for long-term leasing have realized important benefits from that privilege and this opportunity should now be extended to all Indian tribes.

Fostering Indian Economic Growth

Economic planning is another area where our efforts can be significantly improved. The comprehensive economic development plans that have been created by both the Pima-Maricopa and the Zuni Tribes provide outstanding examples of interagency cooperation in fostering Indian economic growth. The Zuni Plan, for example, extends for at least five years and involves a total of $55 million from the Departments of Interior, Housing and Urban Development, and Health, Education and Welfare and from the Office of Economic Opportunity and the Economic Development Administration. I am directing the Secretary of the Interior to play an active role in coordinating additional projects of this kind.

6. *More Money for Indian Health*

Despite significant improvements in the past decade and a half, the health of Indian people still lags 20 to 25 years behind that of the general population. The average age at death among Indians is 44 years, about one-third less than the national average. Infant mortality is nearly 50% higher for Indians and Alaska natives than for the population at large; the tuberculosis rate is eight times as high and the suicide rate is twice that of the general population. Many infectious diseases such as trachoma and dysentery that have all but disappeared among other Americans continue to afflict the Indian people.

This Administration is determined that the health status of the first Americans will be improved. In order to initiate expanded efforts in this area, I will request the allocation of an additional $10 million for Indian health programs for the current fiscal year. This strengthened Federal effort will enable us to address ourselves more effectively to those health problems which are particularly important to the Indian community. We understand, for example, that areas of greatest concern to Indians include the prevention and control of alcoholism, the promotion of mental health and the control of middle-ear disease. We hope that the ravages of middle-ear disease—a particularly acute disease among Indians—can be brought under control within five years.

These and other Indian health programs will be most effective if more Indians are involved in running them. Yet—almost unbelievably—we are presently able to identify in this country only 30 physicians and fewer than 400 nurses of Indian descent. To meet this situation, we will expand our efforts to train Indians for health careers.

7. *Helping Urban Indians*

Our new census will probably show that a larger proportion of America's Indians are living off the reservation than ever before in our history. Some authorities even estimate that more Indians are living in cities and towns than are remaining on the reservation. Of those American Indians who are now dwelling in urban areas, approximately three-fourths are living in poverty.

The Secretary of the Interior and the Attorney General must at the same time advance both *the* national *interest in the use of land and water rights* and *the* private *interests of Indians in land which the government holds as trustee.*

The Bureau of Indian Affairs is organized to serve the 462,000 reservation Indians. The BIA's responsibility does not extend to Indians who have left the reservation, but this point is not always clearly understood. As a result of this misconception, Indians living in urban areas have often lost out on the opportunity to participate in other programs designed for disadvantaged groups. As a first step toward helping the urban Indians, I am instructing appropriate officials to do all they can to ensure that this misunderstanding is corrected.

But misunderstandings are not the most important problem confronting urban Indians. The biggest barrier faced by those Federal, State and local programs which are trying to serve urban Indians is the difficulty of locating and identifying them. Lost in the anonymity of the city, often cut off from family and friends, many urban Indians are slow to establish new community ties. Many drift from neighborhood to neighborhood; many shuttle back and forth between reservations and urban areas. Language and cultural differences compound these problems. As a result, Federal, State and local programs which are designed to help such persons often miss this most deprived and least understood segment of the urban poverty population.

Creating Urban Indian Centers

This Administration is already taking steps which will help remedy this situation. In a joint effort, the Office of Economic Opportunity and the Department of Health, Education and Welfare will expand support to a total of seven urban Indian centers in major cities which will act as links between existing Federal, State and local service programs and the urban Indians. The Departments of Labor, Housing and Urban Development and Commerce have pledged to cooperate with such experimental urban centers and the Bureau of Indian Affairs has expressed its willingness to contract with these centers for the performance of relocation services which assist reservation Indians in their transition to urban employment.

These efforts represent an important beginning in recognizing and alleviating the severe problems faced by urban Indians. We hope to learn a great deal from these projects and to expand our efforts as rapidly as possible. I am directing the Office of Economic Opportunity to lead these efforts. . . .

A New, Coherent Strategy

The recommendations of this Administration represent an historic step forward in Indian policy. We are proposing to break sharply with past approaches to Indian problems. In place of a long series of piecemeal reforms, we suggest a new and coherent strategy. In place of policies which simply call for more spending, we suggest policies which call for wiser spending. In place of policies which oscillate between the deadly extremes of forced termination and constant paternalism, we suggest a policy in which the Federal government and the Indian community play complementary roles.

But most importantly, we have turned from the question of *whether* the Federal government has a responsibility to Indians to the question of *how* that responsibility can best be fulfilled. We have concluded that the Indians will get better programs and that public monies will be more effectively expended if the people who are most affected by these programs are responsible for operating them.

The Indians of America need Federal assistance—this much has long been clear. What has not always been clear, however, is that the Federal government needs Indian energies and Indian leadership if its assistance is to be effective in improving the conditions of Indian life. It is a new and balanced relationship between the United States government and the first Americans that is at the heart of our approach to Indian problems. And that is why we now approach these problems with new confidence that they will successfully be overcome.

3

The Reservation Conflict Continues

Donald L. Fixico

What is the state of the Indian Reservation system today? While the self-determination policy established in the last third of the twentieth century continues, so does conflict, both within the reservations themselves and within the larger society. Anthropologist Peter Nabokov writes,

> The focus on cultural revitalization sharpened the old debate within Indian communities over how white to become, and resurrected the question "What is a tribe?" "Is it a traditionally organized band of Indians following customs with medicine men and chief dominating the policies?" as [historian Vine] Deloria [Jr.] phrased the choice before many native groups, "or is it a modern corporate structure attempting to compromise with modern white culture?"

In addition to wrestling with questions of self-identity, the tribes have had to wrestle with various governmental entities, both federal and state. Some state governments still claim legal jurisdiction over Indian activities on and off the reservations in their states. For example, conflict often erupts over who has the right to regulate Indian hunting and fishing. And jurisdiction over reservation crime is still a controversial issue.

Some Indians continue waging the fight for absolute sovereignty over their reservations. But not all agree that this is desirable. Robert Burnette, a member of the South Dakota Rosebud Sioux, says,

> In my estimation, there are only two jurisdictions in the United States. They are state and federal jurisdiction. In-

113

dian tribes happen to be under federal jurisdiction, which is superior to state jurisdiction. If people keep claiming tribal jurisdiction to be a fact, they are bound to lose to states' rights because tribes do not have the population or power to maintain their sovereignty.

Some reservations remain hopelessly mired in poverty and its attendant ills. But some have found ways to successfully exploit the resources at hand. One of the newest strategies reservations have pursued to attain economic success is gaming. In 1987 the Supreme Court rendered a decision that has changed reservation economies more dramatically than any other single decision. In *California v. Cabazon Band of Mission Indians* the Court ruled that Indian tribes may conduct any gaming activities not specifically prohibited by state law. Subsequently, Congress passed the Indian Gaming Regulatory Act, which applied the *Cabazon* ruling to all states, with the stipulation that the tribe and the state must agree on the tribe's plan. Many of the states that have Indian gaming restrict it to the reservations; there is no other legal gambling in the state.

At present, some 130 tribes in 37 states have casinos on their reservations. Some casinos offer only Bingo; others have slot machines and card rooms. On some reservations casinos have become big business and have benefited the entire tribe. The *St. Paul* (Minnesota) *Pioneer Press*, reported in September 2000 that the Shakopee Mdewakanton Dakota Sioux band, for example, had a 69.52 percent unemployment rate in 1991; after the reservation's casino was established, the unemployment rate had dropped to 4 percent by 1997, and each of the 254 enrolled (official) tribe members receives hundreds of thousands of dollars of casino revenue each year.

On other reservations, the benefits, if any, are not widespread. The Associated Press reported in September 2000 that the San Carlos Apache band in San Carlos, Arizona, is a large, impoverished population even after the establishment of a glitzy casino complex. "We get no help from the casino, no money, nothing," states one tribe member.

A number of tribal governments have sought more conventional routes to economic independence. They have bowed to pressures from the government and from large private corporations to lease reservation lands that are rich in increasingly rare resources—coal, oil, timber, grazing land, water. In some cases tribes have reaped substantial royalties from the leases, but often at the cost of significant harm to the land. The Department of the Interior still has the power to approve leases, sometimes bypassing the tribes' will, and sometimes, according to the tribes, negotiating leasing arrangements that benefit energy companies rather than the Indians.

In the following article, historian Donald L. Fixico points out that "it is ironic that today's Indian leaders are negotiating with white Americans and the federal government for tribal lands just as their ancestors did more than one hundred years ago." Fixico, a mixed-blood Indian, is director of the Indigenous Nations Studies Program at the University of Kansas in Lawrence. He has written many articles and several books on American Indian history, including *The Invasion of Indian Country in the Twentieth Century: American Capitalism and Tribal Natural Resources* and *They Never Told Us . . . The Urban Indian Experience in America.*

More than 100 years ago, Indian tribal leaders were forced to negotiate with white Americans and the U.S. government for possession of Indian lands. Today's tribal leaders face a similar situation, due to the growing energy crisis and increased demands for natural resources. Depletion of America's mineral reserves has caused energy companies to look toward reservation lands to replenish needed oil, coal, gas, and uranium supplies. Even water has become a precious resource for transporting coal in slurry pipelines. In almost every Western state, Indian and white interests are competing for this priceless commodity. And as a result of the increasing demand for natural resources, relations between tribal reservation leaders and white Americans have intensified.

Today, more than half of the nation's coalfields are west of the Mississippi River. One-third of the Western fields exist on lands of twenty-two tribes, and large portions of most of these tribes' reservations will be disrupted during mining operations. The Northern Cheyenne, whose 440,000-acre reservation stands over a rich coal vein in southeastern Montana, will have approximately fifty-six percent of their land mined. The Crow Reservation, adjacent to the Cheyenne, will suffer similar disturbances, reducing the land available for the Crow's own use. In Montana and North Dakota, coalfields are estimated to contain fifteen times the energy reserves of the Alaska North Slope oil and gas fields. The Jicarilla Apache Reservation, in New Mexico, contains 154 million barrels of oil and 2 trillion cubic feet of gas. Overall, geologists report that twenty-five to forty percent of America's uranium, one-third of its coal, and approximately five percent of its oil and gas are on Indian reservations in the West.

Mining Has Long Been Done on Reservation Land

Large-scale mining on reservation lands has occurred since the late nineteenth century. In the late 1800s and early decades of the twentieth century, for example, coal was mined on Choctaw and Chickasaw lands in southeastern Oklahoma. Water was vied for on the Fort Belknap Reservation in Montana in the early 1900s, and non-Indians aggressively pursued Pueblo irrigated lands in the 1920s. Oil was pumped from wells on the lands of the Osage, Creek, and Seminole in Oklahoma during the 1920s and 1930s. In the 1950s, tons of coal was mined on the Crow and Northern Cheyenne Reservations in Montana. In the 1960s, Peabody Coal Company and Shell Oil operated coal mines on the Crow Reservation, and the latter made a record bid of $1.1 million for prospecting rights on 83,000 acres of Crow land. In the late 1960s, the Department of the Interior encouraged the Navajo and Hopi tribes to provide water and to forgo taxing non-Indians on their reservations so that a power plant using coal could be built at Page, Arizona. The Bureau of Indian Affairs convinced tribal leaders that nuclear power would replace the need for Indian coal in the area. But in the next few years, the coal industry raced to its highest profits ever, and the Navajo and Hopi were locked into contracts for many years.

Mining operations on Indian lands can be monetarily beneficial; consequently, tribes bestowed with large mineral deposits on their reservations receive large royalty payments. Such revenue enables the tribes to promote various programs and to improve their economies. The Western tribes faced a grave dilemma, however. Should they allow mining development of their reservations? In 1977, Peter MacDonald, chairperson of the Navajo Nation, noted in a speech before the Western attorneys general in Seattle that "the history of Indian resource development reaches far into our past. Before the white man came to our lands, Indians developed their resources for their own needs. Our people used only what they needed, and they were very careful not to destroy the land. The railroads, trucks and powerlines transport this material [resources] off the reservation to provide Americans with a better life. . . . At the same time, most Indians still live in poverty, without such 'luxuries' as water and electricity, which most Americans regard as the barest necessities of life."[1]

Divided Indian Response

The Indians' reaction to the demand for their energy resources is twofold: reluctance to allow the mining operations to continue, on one hand, and a progressive attitude toward increased mining to help develop tribal programs, on the other. Among the Western tribes, factions for and against mining have developed among the Native peoples. Conservative traditionalists oppose mining. Progressives, especially tribal leaders, favor mining, but they are in the minority. Nevertheless, tribal leaders control their tribes' affairs, and they sometimes negotiate with energy companies without their peoples' consent.

Generally, the conservative blocs consist of the tribal elders. They see their traditional cultures threatened, leading them to believe that after the mining companies are gone, their lands will never be the same. David Strange Owl, one of thirty-six Northern Cheyenne on a fact-finding mission, visited the mining operations on the Navajo Reservation in the spring of 1977. He confessed, "Before, I didn't know much about coal." Observing the mining operations aroused in him feelings of repugnance: "What I've seen between the Navajo and Hopi is a sad thing, to see the strip-mining, on their reservations . . . because it's going to hurt a lot of lives of [our] reservation—our lives, our culture."[2] Possessing a deep attachment to the land, traditionalists view themselves as a part of that land. According to Native tradition, the earth is mother to all, and no harm should come to her, in fact, the "Mother Earth" concept is one of the few universal concepts among American Indians. Those who still hold to this concept say that tribal members who want to exploit the land are no longer Indians. . . .

Mining operations are lending credence to the traditionalists' fears. As their machines scar mother earth and jeopardize the relationship between nature and mankind, the companies bring more non-Indians onto the reservation. Soon, the non-Indians may outnumber the Native people on their own lands. If current mining operations continue on the Northern Cheyenne Reservation, for instance, twenty non-Indians will be brought in for every Cheyenne living there. Many Indians charge that tribal leaders are abusing not only their land but also their people and their culture by cooperating with energy companies.

The conservative blocs . . . believe that after the mining companies are gone, their lands will never be the same.

Conversely, tribal leaders believe that they can improve the welfare of their people by generating revenues and funding programs from mining arrangements. They deem that now is the time to take advantage of the energy companies. And with the increasing demand for natural resources, there is no doubt that revenue received from mining companies will mean further changes in Indian lifestyles. For some Native people, social changes are already taking place. Residents of reservations who work at off-reservation jobs, for instance, are familiar with the mainstream society.

The progressive Indian nations have elected to improve their situation socially, politically, and economically. Peter MacDonald asserted that his people have chosen to change: "We are an emerging nation. Like other underdeveloped countries with rich but exhaustible supplies of fuel and minerals, we realize we must use our natural resources to create jobs for our people and put us on the road to economic self-sufficiency. Otherwise, we will not have anything left when our resources are gone. That's why we are demanding more from the people who want to exploit our wealth."[3] . . .

A History of Inadequate Payments

Tribal leaders protest that the royalty payments from leases are too low and that tribes are locked into poorly negotiated leases for long periods of time. Because the secretary of the interior is empowered by law to approve leases, the energy companies can control Indian lands by entering into agreements with the Interior Department. Supposedly, the tribes will benefit from such agreements, but Indians criticize the government for failing to advise tribes correctly and for not protecting them from being victimized. Tribes endowed with energy resources are also angered by the lack of proper supervision by the Bureau of Indian Affairs in protecting Indian interests and by the bureau's urging of tribes to accept inadequate leases.

The Northern Cheyenne have alleged that from 1969 to 1971, the U.S. government misadvised them repeatedly. During this period, Peabody, Amax, and Chevron were given exploration and mining leases for over half of the reservation's 450,000 acres. The tribe did not realize how unfair the ill-advised agreements were until 1972, when Consolidation Coal Company offered the tribe $35 an acre, a royalty rate of $.25 per ton of coal, and a $1.5 million community health center. After further investigation, the Cheyenne Tribal Council charged the federal government with thirty-six violations of leasing procedures.

The tribe petitioned Rogers Morton, then secretary of the interior, to cancel all of their leases with energy companies. Instead, the secretary suspended the leases until a "mutual agreement" was worked out between the companies and the tribe. But the Northern Cheyenne demanded cancellation. "We don't negotiate with the companies until they tear those leases up in front of us and burn them," said tribal chairman Allen Rowland. "And we can start over on our terms, not theirs."[4]

Tribal leaders believe that they can improve the welfare of their people by generating revenues and funding programs from mining arrangements.

Government and industry officials have responded that, although some mistakes have been made, most leases were negotiated fairly. In 1974, Secretary Morton told Northern Cheyenne leaders that they would have to abide by lease agreements with Peabody, Consolidation, and other companies. Later that same year, however, Northern Cheyenne leases were suspended, and leasing was conducted by negotiation or competitive bidding.

The Crow have charged the secretary of the interior

with violating the National Environmental Policy Act and have said that, as a result, their coal leases do not comply with federal regulations. Since the government represents the tribes, through the BIA and the secretary of the interior, there are conflicting attitudes within the federal government, and the tribes are caught in between. The Omnibus Tribal Leasing Act of 1938 authorized the Department of the Interior to approve leases between the tribes and the mining companies. "The government is the trustee of the Indians and the coordinator of national energy policy. That is a conflict of interests," stated Thomas J. Lynaugh, an attorney for the Crow Tribe.[5] Hopi chairperson Abbott Sekaquaptewa summed up the situation when he commented, "The energy situation has put us in a much better posture. We are going to make our decisions on whether to develop our resources, when it will be done, and how."[6]

Indian leaders are currently taking a more active role in the negotiations for their natural resources. In some instances, tribal officials are suing against long-term leases that underpay their tribes, especially because the American dollar has shrunk since these leases were originally signed. . . .

Indians Have Organized

In an effort to protect reservation resources, leaders of twenty-five Western Indian tribes united in 1975 to form the Council of Energy Resource Tribes (CERT). CERT is controlled by an executive board consisting of eight tribal chairpersons and a ninth chairperson who serves as the executive director. With one-third of all coal in the West located on Indian lands, CERT takes an aggressive business approach toward energy firms to bargain in the best interests of the tribes. It sought advice in the late 1970s from several members of the Organization of Petroleum Exporting Countries (OPEC) over the U.S. government's disapproval. To halt further OPEC assistance, the federal government awarded CERT grants totaling $1,997,000 from the Department of Energy (DOE), the BIA, and the Department of Health, Education, and Welfare. Initially, CERT opened offices in Denver, Colorado, and Washington, D.C., but it closed the doors of the Washington office when its 1982 budget of $6 million was cut to $3.1 million in 1983. The council educates tribes in evaluating their energy sources, in the technology of mining natural resources, and in the development of human resources; it also provides management studies and computer services. To prevent further exploitation of Indian lands, CERT has established a broad Indian policy "so that energy companies won't be able to pick us off one by one," according to Charles Lohah, the acting secretary for CERT.[7]

Indian leaders are currently taking a more active role in the negotiations for their natural resources.

It should be added that despite its success, the organization has hardly been immune from criticism. In recent years, CERT has been severely criticized by Indians who charge that it is too "pro-development" regarding reservation resources. CERT has also been accused of holding "glittery, black-tie galas for federal officials and energy company brass."[8]

Many Mineral Corporations Have Presence on Reservations

The list of corporations on Indian lands in the West is long. In the Black Hills of South Dakota alone, 26 multinational corporations have obtained state prospecting leases for over one million acres. Other examples include several energy companies working in the Four Corners area on the Navajo and Hopi Reservations, mining for coal and uranium. In Oklahoma, the Sac and Fox, Osage, Creek, Choctaw, Chickasaw, and other tribes have leases with energy companies extracting oil, gas, or coal.

Until recent years, energy firms have had easy access to Western coalfields. The Department of the Interior could persuade tribal officials to lease lands to companies, thereby easing the exploitation of Indian lands. As a result, the Utah International Mining Company has been operating the largest strip-mining project in the world in the Four Corners region on Navajo land. In response to growing pressure to renegotiate with the Crow Tribe, Westmoreland Resources renegotiated its mining leases with the Crow in November 1973. The Crow Tribe formed the Crow Mineral Committee, which was elected by the tribal council and entrusted to negotiate directly with Westmoreland officials. As of 1975, of the entire Crow Reservation of 2,226,000 acres, Westmoreland leased 30,876 acres, Shell Oil leased 30,248 acres, Peabody Coal leased 86,122 acres, and Gulf Minerals Resources leased 73,292 acres. A 1975 survey prepared by Rural Research Associates of Missoula and Edgar, Montana, estimated that the Crow Reservation contained four to five and a half billion tons of strippable coal, plus six to twelve billion tons of coal that would be more costly to mine.

Indians Are Learning the Business

Today, as Native American officials who conduct negotiations with energy company officials, tribal leaders are developing a new image for themselves. Unlike their forebears, today's tribal leaders understand the complexities of handling land negotiations. Company and government officials have noticed the transition from the old tribal leadership; the new leaders are adamant in their demands and cognizant of white ways of dealing for land.

Reservation leaders have become more successful in negotiations, and the future looks brighter for Plains and Southwest tribes. With the increased knowledge and understanding of white ways, tribal leaders are also initiating and developing new programs to help their people. In this context, it is appropriate to cite the advice of the Sioux leader Sitting Bull. When the mighty Sioux Nation was in decline, mostly because of white influence, Sitting Bull warned: "Take the best of the white man's road, pick it up and take it with you. That which is bad, leave it alone, cast it away. Take the best of the old Indian ways—always keep them. They have been proven for thousands of years. Do not let them die."[9]

The younger tribal leaders of the Western reservations are making tremendous strides in improving the tribes' status. Beginning at the level of Third World nations, Indian groups are progressing rapidly toward parity with white American society. With competent leadership and additional aid from the Bureau of Indian Affairs, energy tribes have been able to develop successful industries. Federal funds have been appropriated to finance such tribal ventures as Yatay Industries, Sandia Indian Industries, Apache Indian Industries, and Ute Fabricating, Ltd. Other tribal industries include Northern Pueblo Enterprises, Navajo Indian Wood Products, Zuni Enterprises, and White Eagle Industries. These business ventures are the result of careful planning, and they exemplify the entrepreneurial quality of modern Indian achievement. . . .

Many tribal leaders and reservation peoples, however, face serious problems. Some Americans assume that Indians are getting rich from royalty payments, though actually only fifteen percent of the Indian population has natural resources on tribal lands. In 1982, the BIA reported that royalties on reservations totaled more than $396 million, but if the royalties were distributed to the entire Indian population of 1.3 million (according to the 1980 census), the per capita payment would be only $290 for each person. For their oil, tribes received on the average $2 a barrel in royalties at a time when OPEC nations were demanding and receiving $40 a barrel. Four of the largest energy resource deposits are on the Blackfeet, Crow, Fort Peck, and Wind River Reservations in Montana and Wyoming. In 1980, more than 1,200 wells on the four Plains reservations produced 6.1 million barrels of oil. As for coal, in early 1981, when American coal was being sold to foreign buyers for $70 a ton, the Navajo were receiving only $.15 a ton from Utah International Mining Company and less than $.38 a ton from Pittsburgh and Midway Coal Company. These two companies negotiated leases with the Navajos in 1953, 1964, and 1966. . . .

Business Values Conflict with Tradition

Today's tribal leaders, unlike their ancestors, have had to adopt a hurried "get-tough" attitude in a businesslike, modern, "ruthless" way. Such behavior is foreign to the traditional nature of Indian leadership, and it is an obstacle that tribal representatives must overcome if their people are to survive. Although the leaders can probably use more expertise in running their reservation governments like corporations, they know how to hire such expertise. In a very short time, they have become educated in the high-finance business world, and they are experienced in dealing with the bureaucracy of the federal government. Contemporary Indian leaders are sophisticated and forceful in order to protect their people and their reservations—lands that were deemed worthless in the nineteenth century.

The energy crises and the industrial demand for natural resources on Indian lands imply serious repercussions for the tribes' future. The anticipated outcomes are both positive and negative and will have tremendous impact on Indian leaders, tribal members, and reservation lands. The mining operations, the gasification plants to convert coal into gas, and the facilities necessary to produce electricity are extensive and cover large areas of land; as a result, reservation supplies of nonreplaceable natural resources are being severely depleted. In addition, land formations that have religious significance to the people are permanently damaged. Even with reclamation attempts to restore the land to its original state, it will never be the same to the traditional Indian.

For their oil, tribes receive on the average $2 a barrel in royalties at a time when OPEC nations were demanding and receiving $40 a barrel.

Perhaps the fears of the tribal elders who oppose the mining of their mother earth are justified. While tribal leaders are trying to improve their tribes' economies through new programs, schools, and jobs, perhaps a greater harm will come to their people. Aside from the exploitation of their lands, the trend to adopt white ways may also mean that much of the tribal cultures will be forgotten.

Can Indians live with one foot in the traditional world and the other in the white world? Many are doing it now, but how much of their tribal heritage do they remember, and how successfully have they assimilated into white American society? Currently, more Indians than ever are receiving the same education as whites and are moving rapidly into the mainstream society. Indians who live on reservations are becoming more aware of the functions of white society as they travel to and from their reservations. Once living in poverty, many Native people have now raised their economic level and have become successful American citizens according to white standards. Perhaps it is premature to judge whether the Indian has opted for social change at the cost of losing Native identity. Certainly, the next generation will provide better answers.

Notes

1. "Energy and Land Use Questions on Indian Lands," *Wassaja* 5, no. 6 (September 1977), originally stated in "A Major Statement to the Annual Meeting of Western Attorney Generals," Seattle, Washington, August 9, 1977, by former Navajo chairperson Peter MacDonald.
2. "Killing the Earth, Air, Water," *Akwesasne Notes* 9, no. 1 (Spring 1977).
3. "American Indians Bargain 'Arab Style' to Cash in on Resources," *U.S. News and World Report*, June 3, 1974, p. 53.
4. "The Northern Cheyenne . . . 'Defending the Last Retreat'. . ." *Akwesasne Notes* 10, no. 1 (Spring 1978).
5. "A Crow Threat," *Akwesasne Notes* 2, no. 2 (May 1979).
6. "Indians Want a Bigger Share of Their Wealth," *Business Week*, May 3, 1976, p. 100.
7. "Indians Want a Bigger Share of Their Wealth," p. 101.
8. John A. Farrell, "Empty Promises, Misplaced Trust," New Indian War Series, *Denver Post*, November 20, 1983.
9. Fred Harris and LaDonna Harris, "Indians, Coal, and the Big Sky," *The Progressive* (December 1974), p. 22.

Chronology

1492

Christopher Columbus's landing on Hispaniola (now the Dominican Republic) sets the stage for European exploitation of the New World and its native inhabitants.

1619

The Jamestown colonists establish a school for Indian children in order to convert them to Christianity.

1633

Massachusetts Colony establishes a government committee to deal with Indian issues.

1638

The Puritans establish the first Indian reservation, taking all Indian land in what is now Connecticut—except the twelve hundred acres of the reservation—and requiring the Indians to submit to various trade, religious, and other restrictions.

1737

Thomas Penn (son of William) discovers an alleged old agreement with the Delaware Indians stating that the Pennsylvania settlers could own all of the lands around the Delaware River that a man could walk in a day and a half; a carefully planned "walk" allows the settlers to acquire twelve hundred square miles of Delaware lands, forcing the Delawares to move to refugee areas in western Pennsylvania.

1778

The first U.S.-Indian treaty is signed.

1779

George Washington sends four thousand troops to attack Iroquois villages.

1784

The United States forces a treaty upon the New York Iroquois, requiring them to give up their lands in New York, Pennsylvania, Ohio, and Kentucky and move to a small reservation in New York State. In the following sixty-five years, more treaties are signed with more tribes, nearly all including Indian land cessions to the settlers and many forcing the Indians to move to small plots reserved for them. These treaties—many of them achieved by trickery—plus additional land purchases, put 450 million acres of Indian lands into the hands of the U.S. government and white settlers.

1824
Secretary of War John C. Calhoun establishes the Bureau of Indian Affairs.

1828
The state of Georgia passes its Indian Removal Bill, designed to put the Cherokee entirely under Georgia's jurisdiction and to remove the tribe from its lands.

1830
Congress passes the Indian Removal Law, requiring all southern Indian tribes to be moved west of the Mississippi and establishing Indian Territory in what is now Oklahoma, Arkansas, and Kansas.

1837
Congress decides that Indians will no longer be paid directly for lands bought from them; instead, the money will be held "in trust" in the U.S. Treasury and be used for the benefit of the Indians.

1848
Gold is discovered in California; white miners invade the state in phenomenal numbers, overrunning Indian lands and wiping out thousands of Indians.

1853
Colonel Kit Carson drives the Navajo from their Arizona lands, sending them on "the Long Walk" through more than 350 miles of winter and spring blizzards to Bosque Redondo, New Mexico.

1861
The Civil War begins; many Indians side with the Confederacy, which promises to respect Indian sovereignty.

1864
Gold discoveries in Colorado prompt the Sand Creek Massacre, in which seven hundred U.S. government troops murder nearly two hundred peaceful Cheyenne, mostly women,

children, and elderly men, while the Indians are encamped, waiting to negotiate with the government. Later gold discoveries in Montana, South Dakota, and elsewhere lead to further land skirmishes and Indian removals.

1869

The transcontinental railroad bulldozes through reserved Indian lands, displacing and angering the Indians.

1870

Congress passes a law forbidding army officers from being Indian agents, so President Ulysses S. Grant puts the Indian agencies under Christian missionary control.

1871

Congress signs a bill stating that no further treaties will be signed with Indians; all future agreements will be made by government decree.

1876

The Sioux lose the gold-laden Black Hills to the government and are forced onto reservations.

1878

The Hampton Institute in Virginia becomes the first off-reservation Indian boarding school. Its mission, like that of the schools that followed, is to wipe out the "Indian" in its students and make them into "white men"; students are allowed to speak only English and are forced to practice Christian rituals, dress like white people, and learn "white" trades—farming, milling, and teaching, for example.

1882

President Chester Arthur establishes a four-thousand-square-mile Hopi reservation in northern Arizona.

1887

Congress passes the Dawes Act, or General Allotment Act, to end the reservation system and tribal landholding.

1889

The Ghost Dance religion is revived; Plains Indians believe that this religion will make white people disappear from the land; instead, whites panic at the thought of an Indian uprising and massacre hundreds of Indians at Wounded Knee, South Dakota, in 1890; the government opens unoccupied land in Indian Territory to settlers, leading to the Oklahoma land rush in which more than fifty thousand white settlers move onto Indian lands.

1903
The Supreme Court decision in *Wolf v. Hitchcock* gives Congress the power to ignore or change Indian treaties.

1907
Congress gives Bureau of Indian Affairs commissioner Francis Leupp the power to sell all allotments belonging to "noncompetents," which Leupp interprets to mean anyone who has not "properly" developed his land.

1910
Congress opens more than thirty western reservations to allotment and sale.

1919
All Indians who served in World War I are granted U.S. citizenship.

1922
Oil is discovered on the Navajo reservation; Interior Secretary Albert Fall manipulates the law to allow the government to lease the oil lands to Standard Oil of California.

1924
Indians are made citizens of the United States.

1928
The Meriam Report documents the impact of allotment on Indian tribes: a shocking increase in poverty, disease, and mortality rate.

1934
The Indian Reorganization Act protects tribes' current land base and permits tribes to establish independent tribal governments with specific rights and responsibilities in relation to the federal government; it also encourages the development of tribal culture and crafts.

1942
The government establishes Japanese internment camps on Pima and Mohave Indian reservations, taking nearly 1.5 million acres of Indian land in Arizona, Alaska, and South Dakota for use in the war effort as internment camps, gunnery ranges, and nuclear test sites.

1949

The Hoover Commission (headed by former president Herbert Hoover) recommends that the federal government end its responsibility for Indian affairs; in addition to terminating government services, the policy would remove the nontax status for Indian-held lands, encourage Indians to leave their reservations to seek employment in cities, and open up Indian lands for mineral exploitation.

1968

The American Indian Movement is founded; during a general period of civil rights activism, this group and others bring public attention to Indian issues.

1970

President Richard Nixon formally ends the termination policy, replacing it with a policy of Indian self-determination—that is, tribes once again are given autonomy over many civil and criminal matters and are encouraged to build strong, self-ruled tribal governments.

During the rest of the twentieth century, Indian issues revolve largely around Indians' rights vis à vis mineral deposits (coal, oil, gold, uranium) on reservation land, Indians' self-determination rights, the issue of reservation sovereignty, relations with federal and state governments, and economic struggles.

For Further Research

Books
William L. Anderson, ed., *Cherokee Removal: Before and After*. Athens: University of Georgia Press, 1991.
Robert L. Bee, *The Politics of American Indian Policy*. Cambridge, MA: Schenkman, 1982.
Christine Bolt, *American Indian Policy and American Reform: Case Studies of the Campaign to Assimilate the American Indian*. London: Allen & Unwin, 1987.
Henry Warner Bowden, *American Indians and Christian Missions: Studies in Cultural Conflict*. Chicago: University of Chicago Press, 1981.
Dee Brown, *Bury My Heart at Wounded Knee: An Indian History of the American West*. New York: Bantam Books, 1970.
William C. Canby Jr., *American Indian Law in a Nutshell*. St. Paul: West, 1981.
Henry B. Carrington, *The Indian Question, Including a Report by the Secretary of the Interior on the Massacre of Troops Near Fort Kearny, December 1866*. New York: Sol Lewis, 1973.
Confederation of American Indians, comp., *Indian Reservations: A State and Federal Handbook*. Jefferson, NC: McFarland, 1985.
Rupert Costo and Jeannette Henry, *Indian Treaties: Two Centuries of Dishonor*. San Francisco: Indian Historian, 1977.
Jefferson Davis and Albert Pike, *Message of the President and Report of Albert Pike, Commissioner of the Confederate States to the Indian Nations West of Arkansas, of the Results of His Mission*. Richmond, VA: Enquirer Book and Job, 1861.
Angie Debo, *A History of the Indians of the United States*. Norman: University of Oklahoma Press, 1984.
————, *The Road to Disappearance*. Norman: University of Oklahoma Press, 1941.
Carl N. Degler, *Assimilation vs. Separation*. Washington, DC: U.S. Information Agency, 1973.

Vine Deloria Jr., ed., *American Indian Policy in the Twentieth Century.* Norman: University of Oklahoma Press, 1985.

Vine Deloria Jr. and Clifford M. Lytle, *The Nations Within: The Past and Future of Indian Sovereignty.* 1984. Reprint, Austin: University of Texas Press, 1998.

Vine Deloria Jr. and Raymond DeMaljie, eds., *Proceedings of the Great Peace Commission of 1867–1868.* Washington, DC: Institute for the Development of Indian Law, 1975.

Arthur H. DeRosier Jr., *The Removal of the Choctaw Indians.* Knoxville: University of Tennessee Press, 1970.

Brian W. Dippie, *The Vanishing American: White Attitudes and U.S. Indian Policy.* Lawrence: University of Kansas Press, 1982.

Economic Development in American Indian Reservations. Albuquerque: University of New Mexico Press, 1979.

Carlos B. Embry, *America's Concentration Camps.* New York: David McKay, 1956.

Louis Filler and Allen Guttmann, eds., *The Removal of the Cherokee Nation: Manifest Destiny or National Dishonor?* Huntington, NY: Robert E. Krieger, 1977.

Donald L. Fixico, *The Invasion of the Indian Country in the Twentieth Century.* Niwot: University Press of Colorado, 1998.

Sarah Winnemucca Hopkins, *Life Among the Piutes: Their Wrongs and Claims.* Reno: University of Nevada Press, 1994.

Bruce E. Johansen, *Shapers of the Great Debate on Native American: Land, Spirit, and Power, a Biographical Dictionary.* Westport, CT: Greenwood, 2000.

Lawrence C. Kelly, *The Assault on Assimilation: John Collier and the Origins of Indian Reform Policy.* Albuquerque: University of New Mexico Press, 1983.

Janet A. McDonnell, *The Dispossession of the American Indian, 1887–1934.* Bloomington: Indiana University Press, 1991.

Thomas L. McKenney, *Memoirs, Official and Personal.* Lincoln: University of Nebraska Press, 1973.

George W. Manypenny, *Our Indian Wards.* 1880. Reprint, New York: Da Capo, 1972.

Robert Winston Mardock, *The Reformers and the American Indian.* Columbia, MO: University Press, 1971.

For Further Research   133

Howard Meredith, *Modern American Indian Tribal Government and Politics*. Tsaile, AZ: Navajo Community College Press, 1993.
James Mooney, *Mooney's History, Myths, and Sacred Formulas of the Cherokees*. Asheville, NC: Historical Images, 1992.
Wayne Moquin and Charles Van Doren, eds., *Great Documents in American Indian History*. 1973. Reprint, New York: Praeger, 1995.
Peter Nabakov, ed., *Native American Testimony: A Chronicle of Indian-White Relations from Prophecy to the Present, 1492–1992*. New York: Penguin Books, 1991.
Judith Nies, *Native American History: A Chronology of a Culture's Vast Achievements and Their Links to World Events*. New York: Ballantine, 1996.
Kenneth R. Philip, *Termination Revisited: American Indians on the Trail to Self-Determination, 1933–1953*. Lincoln: University of Nebraska Press, 1999.
Kenneth R. Philip, ed., *Indian Self-Rule: First-Hand Accounts of Indian-White Relations from Roosevelt to Reagan*. Salt Lake City: Institute of the American West, 1986.
Albert Pike, *Message of the President and Report of Albert Pike, Commissioner of the Confederate States to the Indian Nations West of Arkansas, of the Results of His Mission*. Richmond, VA: Enquirer Book and Job, 1861.
Loring Benson Priest, *Uncle Sam's Stepchildren: The Reformation of United States Indian Policy, 1865–1887*. New Brunswick, NJ: Rutgers University Press, 1942.
Francis Paul Prucha, *American Indian Policy in the Formative Years: The Indian Trade and Intercourse Acts, 1790–1834*. Lincoln: University of Nebraska Press, 1970.
————, *Indian Policy in the United States*. Lincoln: University of Nebraska Press, 1981.
Francis Paul Prucha, ed., *Americanizing the American Indians: Writings by the "Friends of the Indian," 1880–1900*. Cambridge, MA: Harvard University Press, 1973.
————, ed., *Documents of United States Indian Policy*. Lincoln: University of Nebraska Press, 1975.
The Removal of the Cherokee. Cherokee, NC: Museum of the Cherokee Indian, n.d.
Theodore Roosevelt, *The Winning of the West: An Account of the Exploration and Settlement of Our Country from the Alleghenies to the Pacific*. New York: Charles Scribner's Sons, 1926.

Annette Rosenstiel, *Red and White: Indian View of the White Man, 1492–1982.* New York: Universe Books, 1983.
Luther Standing Bear, *My People the Sioux.* New York: Houghton Mifflin, 1928.
Stan Steiner, *The New Indians.* New York: Dell, 1968.
Margaret Connell Szasz, ed., *Between Indian and White Worlds: The Culture Broker.* Norman: University of Oklahoma Press, 1994.
Robert A. Trennent Jr., *Alternative to Extinction: Federal Indian Policy and the Beginnings of the Reservation System, 1846–51.* Philadelphia: Temple, 1975.
W.C. Vanderwerth, *Indian Oratory: Famous Speeches by Noted Indian Chieftans.* Norman: University of Oklahoma Press, 1971.
Herman J. Viola, *Thomas L. McKenney: Architect of America's Early Indian Policy, 1816–1830.* Chicago: Swallow/ SAGE Books, 1974.
James Wilson, *The Earth Shall Weep: A History of Native America.* New York: Grove, 1998.
David J. Wishart, *An Unspeakable Sadness: The Dispossession of the Nebraska Indians.* Lincoln: University of Nebraska Press, 1994.

Government Documents

An Act Making Appropriations for the Current and Contingent Expenses of the Indian Department, and for Fulfilling Treaty Stipulations with Various Indian Tribes, for the Year Ending June the Thirtieth, One Thousand Eight Hundred and Fifty-Two, 31st Cong., 2d sess., February 27, 1851.
An Act to Conserve and Develop Indian Lands and Resources; to Extend to Indians the Right to Form Business and Other Organizations; to Establish a Credit System for Indians; to Grant Certain Rights of Home Rule to Indians; to Provide for Vocational Education for Indians; and for Other Purposes, 73rd Cong., 2d sess., June 18, 1934.
An Act to Provide for an Exchange of Lands with the Indians Residing in Any of the States or Territories, and for Their Removal West of the River Mississippi, 21st Cong., 1st sess., May 28, 1830.
An Act to Provide for the Allotment of Lands in Severalty to Indians on the Various Reservations, and to Extend the Protection of the Laws of the United States and the Territories over the Indians, and for Other Purposes, 49th Cong., 2d sess., February 8, 1887.

J.D.C. Atkins, *Report of the Secretary of the Interior,* House Executive Document 1, Part 5, 50th Cong., 1st sess., 1887.

R. Clum, *Report of the Commissioner of Indian Affairs,* November 15, 1871.

Vincent Colyer, *Third Annual Report of the Board of Indian Commissioners to the President,* December 12, 1871.

Jacob D. Cox, *Report of the Secretary of the Interior,* Executive Document 1, Part 3, 41st Cong., 2d sess., Washington, DC: Government Printing Office, 1869.

William P. Dole, *Report of the Commissioner of Indian Affairs,* November 26, 1862.

J.R. Doolittle, *Condition of the Indian Tribes: Report of the Joint Special Committee, with Appendix,* Senate Report No. 156, 39th Cong., 2d sess., 1867.

D.W.C. Duncan, "Statement of Mr. D.W.C. Duncan, a Cherokee Indian", November 14, 1906, Senate Report No. 5013, 59th Cong., 2d sess., Part 1.

Theodore Frelinghuysen, "Remarks, April 9, 1830," *Register of Debates in Congress.* Vol. 6, Part 1. Washington, DC: Gales and Seaton, 1830.

R.W. Johnson, *Report from the Committee on Territories, to Whom Was Referred the Bill to Establish and Organize the Territories of Cha-lah-kee, Muscogee, and Cha-ta,* 33rd Cong., 1st sess., Report Committee No. 379, July 28, 1854.

Wilson Lumpkin, "Remarks on the Removal of the Indians, May 17, 1830," *Register of Debates in Congress.* Vol. 6, Part 2, Washington, DC: Gales and Seaton, 1830.

Charles E. Mix, *Report of the Commissioner of Indian Affairs,* November 6, 1858.

James Monroe, "To the Senate and House of Representatives of the United States, January 27, 1825," in James D. Richardson, *A Compilation of the Messages and Papers of the Presidents, 1789–1897.* Vol. 2. Washington, DC: Government Printing Office, 1896.

Thomas J. Morgan, *Report of the Secretary of the Interior.* Vol. 2, October 1, 1889, House Executive Document 1, 51st Cong., 1st sess., Serial 2725.

Richard Nixon, "Special Message on Indian Affairs, July 8, 1970," *Public Papers of the Presidents of the United States: Richard Nixon,* 1970. Washington, DC: Government Printing Office, 1971.

E.S. Parker, *Annual Report of the Commissioner of Indian Af-*

fairs to the Secretary, March 15, 1871.
Richard Peters, *Reports of Cases Argued and Adjudged in the Supreme Court of the United States, January Term 1832.* Vol. 6. Philadelphia: T. Desilver, 1832.

Periodicals

Lewis Cass, "Documents and Proceedings Relating to the Formation and Progress of a Board in the City of New York, for the Emigration, Preservation, and Improvement of the Aborigines of America," *North American Review*, January 1830.

Hamlin Garland, "The Red Man's Present Needs," *North American Review*, April 1902.

Young Joseph, "An Indian's Views of Indian Affairs," *North American Review*, April 1879.

Nelson A. Miles, "The Indian Problem," *North American Review*, March 1879.

David Pace, "Majority of American Indians Don't Get Benefit from Casinos," *St. Paul Pioneer Press*, September 1, 2000.

Carl Schurz, "Present Aspects of the Indian Problem," *North American Review*, July 1881.

Internet Sources

Gary Gerstle, "Theodore Roosevelt and the Divided Character of American Nationalism." www.history cooperative.org/journals/jah/86.3/gerstle.html.

Nathan Glazer, "American Epic: Then and Now." www.thepublicinterest.com/notable/article5.html.

Eric Mayer, "Land Conflicts." http://emayzine.com/lectures/Native/20Lecture/20Land/20DisputeOverview.htm.

National Gambling Impact Study Commission, "Native American Gaming." www.ngisc.gov/research/nagaming.html.

Native American timeline. www.heard.org/education/resource/htl/html.

Robert Porter, "Strengthening Tribal Government Through Government Reform: What Are the Issues?" www.socwel.ukans.edu/culturaljustice/strtribe.htm.

John Poupart, "Indians Must Face New Wave of Threats to Sovereignty Together," American Indian Research and Policy Institute. www.airpi.org/exespr96.html.

Index